Photoshop CS5 Advanced

Student Manual

ACA Edition

Photoshop CS5: Advanced, ACA Edition

President, Axzo Press:	Jon Winder
Vice President, Product Development:	Charles G. Blum
Vice President, Operations:	Josh Pincus
Director of Publishing Systems Development:	Dan Quackenbush
Writer:	Chris Hale
Copyeditor:	Catherine Oliver
Keytester:	Cliff Coryea

Trademarks

ILT Series is a trademark of Axzo Press.

Some of the product names and company names used in this book have been used for identification purposes only and may be trademarks or registered trademarks of their respective manufacturers and sellers.

Disclaimers

We reserve the right to revise this publication and make changes from time to time in its content without notice.

The Adobe Approved Certification Courseware logo is either a registered trademark or trademark of Adobe Systems Incorporated in the United States and/or other countries. The Adobe Approved Certification Courseware logo is a proprietary trademark of Adobe. All rights reserved.

The ILT Series is independent from ProCert Labs, LLC and Adobe Systems Incorporated, and are not affiliated with ProCert Labs and Adobe in any manner. This publication may assist students to prepare for an Adobe Certified Expert exam, however, neither ProCert Labs nor Adobe warrant that use of this material will ensure success in connection with any exam.

Student Manual
ISBN 10: 1-4260-2075-9
ISBN 13: 978-1-4260-2075-9

Student Manual with Disc
ISBN-10: 1-4260-2077-5
ISBN-13: 978-1-4260-2077-3

Printed in the United States of America
1 2 3 4 5 6 7 8 9 10 GL 13 12 11

Contents

Introduction

After reading this introduction, you will know how to:

A Use ILT Series manuals in general.

B Use prerequisites, a target student description, course objectives, and a skills inventory to properly set your expectations for the course.

C Re-key this course after class.

Topic A: About the manual

ILT Series philosophy

Our manuals facilitate your learning by providing structured interaction with the software itself. While we provide text to explain difficult concepts, the hands-on activities are the focus of our courses. By paying close attention as your instructor leads you through these activities, you will learn the skills and concepts effectively.

We believe strongly in the instructor-led class. During class, focus on your instructor. Our manuals are designed and written to facilitate your interaction with your instructor, and not to call attention to manuals themselves.

We believe in the basic approach of setting expectations, delivering instruction, and providing summary and review afterwards. For this reason, lessons begin with objectives and end with summaries. We also provide overall course objectives and a course summary to provide both an introduction to and closure on the entire course.

Manual components

The manuals contain these major components:

- Table of contents
- Introduction
- Units
- Appendix
- Course summary
- Glossary
- Index

Each element is described below.

Table of contents

The table of contents acts as a learning roadmap.

Introduction

The introduction contains information about our training philosophy and our manual components, features, and conventions. It contains target student, prerequisite, objective, and setup information for the specific course.

Units

Units are the largest structural component of the course content. A unit begins with a title page that lists objectives for each major subdivision, or topic, within the unit. Within each topic, conceptual and explanatory information alternates with hands-on activities. Units conclude with a summary comprising one paragraph for each topic, and an independent practice activity that gives you an opportunity to practice the skills you've learned.

The conceptual information takes the form of text paragraphs, exhibits, lists, and tables. The activities are structured in two columns, one telling you what to do, the other providing explanations, descriptions, and graphics.

Appendix

The appendix for this course lists the Adobe Certified Associate (ACA) exam objectives for Photoshop CS5, along with references to corresponding coverage in ILT Series courseware.

Course summary

This section provides a text summary of the entire course. It is useful for providing closure at the end of the course. The course summary also indicates the next course in this series, if there is one, and lists additional resources you might find useful as you continue to learn about the software.

Glossary

The glossary provides definitions for all of the key terms used in this course.

Index

The index at the end of this manual makes it easy for you to find information about a particular software component, feature, or concept.

Manual conventions

We've tried to keep the number of elements and the types of formatting to a minimum in the manuals. This aids in clarity and makes the manuals more classically elegant looking. But there are some conventions and icons you should know about.

Item	Description
Italic text	In conceptual text, indicates a new term or feature.
Bold text	In unit summaries, indicates a key term or concept. In an independent practice activity, indicates an explicit item that you select, choose, or type.
`Code font`	Indicates code or syntax.
`Longer strings of ▶` `code will look ▶` `like this.`	In the hands-on activities, any code that's too long to fit on a single line is divided into segments by one or more continuation characters (▶). This code should be entered as a continuous string of text.
Select **bold item**	In the left column of hands-on activities, bold sans-serif text indicates an explicit item that you select, choose, or type.
Keycaps like (↵ ENTER)	Indicate a key on the keyboard you must press.

Hands-on activities

The hands-on activities are the most important parts of our manuals. They are divided into two primary columns. The "Here's how" column gives short instructions to you about what to do. The "Here's why" column provides explanations, graphics, and clarifications. Here's a sample:

Do it!

A-1: Creating a commission formula

Here's how	Here's why
1 Open Sales	This is an oversimplified sales compensation worksheet. It shows sales totals, commissions, and incentives for five sales reps.
2 Observe the contents of cell F4	F4 ▼ = =E4*C_Rate The commission rate formulas use the name "C_Rate" instead of a value for the commission rate.

For these activities, we have provided a collection of data files designed to help you learn each skill in a real-world business context. As you work through the activities, you will modify and update these files. Of course, you might make a mistake and therefore want to re-key the activity starting from scratch. To make it easy to start over, you will rename each data file at the end of the first activity in which the file is modified. Our convention for renaming files is to add the word "My" to the beginning of the file name. In the above activity, for example, a file called "Sales" is being used for the first time. At the end of this activity, you would save the file as "My sales," thus leaving the "Sales" file unchanged. If you make a mistake, you can start over using the original "Sales" file.

In some activities, however, it might not be practical to rename the data file. If you want to retry one of these activities, ask your instructor for a fresh copy of the original data file.

Topic B: **Setting your expectations**

Properly setting your expectations is essential to your success. This topic will help you do that by providing:

- Prerequisites for this course
- A description of the target student
- A list of the objectives for the course
- A skills assessment for the course

Course prerequisites

Before taking this course, you should be familiar with personal computers and the use of a keyboard and a mouse. Furthermore, this course assumes that you've completed the following courses or have equivalent experience:

- *Windows 7: Basic*
- *Photoshop CS5: Basic, ACA Edition*

Target student

The target student for this course is familiar with the basics of using Adobe Photoshop to create and modify digital images, and wants to learn additional techniques for creating image effects.

Adobe ACA certification

This course is designed to help you pass the Adobe Certified Associate (ACA) exam for Photoshop CS5. For complete certification training, you should complete this course and all of the following:

- *Photoshop CS5: Basic, ACA Edition*
- *Photoshop CS5: Production, ACA Edition*

Course objectives

These overall course objectives will give you an idea about what to expect from the course. It is also possible that they will help you see that this course is not the right one for you. If you think you either lack the prerequisite knowledge or already know most of the subject matter to be covered, you should let your instructor know that you think you are misplaced in the class.

Note: In addition to the general objectives listed below, specific ACA exam objectives are listed at the beginning of most topics. For a complete mapping of ACA objectives to ILT Series content, see Appendix A.

After completing this course, you will know how to:

* Specify colors and store them in the Swatches panel; apply colors to image selections and as fill layers; apply fill types such as patterns and gradients; use the Preset Manager to save presets; and use overlay layer styles to apply colors and gradients to layer content.

* Paint in Quick Mask mode and in an alpha channel to specify a selection; create a layer mask to hide part of a layer; create grayscale masks to partially mask part of an image; and use a clipping mask to conform one layer to the shape of another.

* Use the path tools and commands to create and edit vector paths; use paths to create vector masks and clipping paths; and use paths to create vector-based artwork.

* Use painting tools, filters, blending modes, and custom brushes to simulate illustrated and painted effects; warp text and layers; group layers and use Smart Objects when creating a composite; edit an image by using the Vanishing Point feature; and apply and mask Smart Filters.

* Use the Actions panel to record, play, and edit actions; display actions as buttons and organize actions into action sets; run an action on multiple images by batch-processing them; and customize keyboard shortcuts and menus.

Skills inventory

Use the following form to gauge your skill level entering the class. For each skill listed, rate your familiarity from 1 to 5, with five being the most familiar. *This is not a test.* Rather, it is intended to provide you with an idea of where you're starting from at the beginning of class. If you're wholly unfamiliar with all the skills, you might not be ready for the class. If you think you already understand all of the skills, you might need to move on to the next course in the series. In either case, you should let your instructor know as soon as possible.

Skill	1	2	3	4	5
Creating swatches					
Filling selections					
Creating fill layers					
Creating gradients					
Creating a simple pattern					
Saving a set of presets					
Creating a tool preset					
Filling areas with overlay layer styles					
Editing a Quick Mask					
Editing an alpha channel as a Quick Mask					
Creating and editing a layer mask					
Working with grayscale masks					
Clipping a layer to an underlying layer					
Creating a type mask					
Understanding the uses of vector paths					
Creating a freeform path					
Converting a selection to a path					
Creating paths with the Pen tool					
Adjusting path points					
Changing the number of anchor points					
Combining subpaths to form a single path					
Creating a vector mask					

Skill	1	2	3	4	5
Converting type characters to editable shapes					
Wrapping type on a path					
Creating a vector shape layer					
Stroking a path with a brush shape					
Simulating an illustration with the Mixer Brush tool					
Blending a texture with Overlay mode					
Creating a custom brush					
Warping text					
Warping image layers					
Using Puppet Warp					
Grouping layers					
Creating and transforming Smart Objects					
Working with Smart Object contents					
Creating vector Smart Objects					
Editing an image with the Vanishing Point filter					
Applying Smart Filters					
Masking Smart Filter effects					
Recording, playing, editing, and pausing an action					
Making actions work as buttons					
Saving actions in sets					
Batch-processing files					
Assigning keyboard shortcuts and menu item colors					

Topic C: Re-keying the course

If you have the proper hardware and software, you can re-key this course after class. This section explains what you'll need in order to do so, and how to do it.

Hardware requirements

Your personal computer should have:

- A keyboard and a mouse
- Intel Pentium 4 or AMD Athlon 64 Processor (or faster)
- 1GB RAM (or higher)
- 1 GB of available hard drive space after the operating system is installed
- A monitor with at least 1280 × 960 resolution

Software requirements

You will also need the following software:

- Microsoft Windows 7 (You can also use Windows Vista or Windows XP, but the screen shots in this course were taken in Windows 7, so your screens might look somewhat different.)
- Adobe Photoshop CS5

Network requirements

The following network components and connectivity are also required for re-keying this course:

- Internet access, for the following purposes:
    - Downloading the latest critical updates and service packs
    - Downloading the Student Data files (if necessary)

Setup instructions to re-key the course

Before you re-key the course, you will need to perform the following steps.

1 Use Windows Update to install all available critical updates and Service Packs.

2 For flat-panel displays, we recommend using the panel's native resolution for best results. Color depth/quality should be set to High (24 bit) or higher.

   Please note that your display settings or resolution may differ from the author's, so your screens might not exactly match the screen shots in this manual.

3 If necessary, reset any Photoshop defaults that you have changed. To do so, when starting Photoshop, hold down Shift+Ctrl+Alt until the dialog box appears, asking if you want to delete the settings file; click Yes. (If you do not wish to reset the defaults, you can still re-key the course, but some activities might not work exactly as documented.)

4 If you have the data disc that came with this manual, locate the Student Data folder on it and copy it to your Windows desktop.

   If you don't have the data disc, you can download the Student Data files for the course:

   a Connect to www.axzopress.com.

   b Under Downloads, click Instructor-Led Training.

   c Browse the subject categories to locate your course. Then click the course title to display a list of available downloads. (You can also access these downloads through our Catalog listings.)

   d Click the link(s) for downloading the Student Data files.

   e Create a folder named Student Data on your Windows desktop.

   f Double-click the downloaded zip file(s) and drag the contents into the Student Data folder.

CertBlaster software

CertBlaster pre- and post-assessment software is available for this course. To download and install this free software, complete the following steps:

1 Go to www.axzopress.com.

2 Under Downloads, click CertBlaster.

3 Click the link for Photoshop CS5.

4 Save the .EXE file to a folder on your hard drive. (**Note:** If you skip this step, the CertBlaster software will not install correctly.)

5 Click Start and choose Run.

6 Click Browse and navigate to the folder that contains the .EXE file.

7 Select the .EXE file and click Open.

8 Click OK and follow the on-screen instructions. When prompted for the password, enter **c_photocs5**.

Unit 1

Fills and overlays

Unit time: 70 minutes

Complete this unit, and you'll know how to:

A Specify colors and store them in the Swatches panel, and apply colors to image selections and as fill layers.

B Apply fill types such as patterns and gradients, and use the Preset Manager to save presets.

C Use overlay layer styles to apply colors and gradients to layer content.

Topic A: Filling image areas

This topic covers the following Adobe ACA exam objectives for Photoshop CS5.

#	Objective
2.1e	Demonstrate knowledge of image optimization with regards to preparing images for web, video, or print.
2.4b	Demonstrate knowledge of appropriate color settings for web, print, and video.
2.5f	Identify the functionality provided by having non-square pixel support when working with video.
3.1c	Demonstrate knowledge of the functions of tools on the Tools panel.
3.1d	Demonstrate knowledge of the functions of various panels.
3.2a	Identify and label elements of the different types of layers.
3.4b	Identify techniques used to produce reusable images.
4.1d	Demonstrate knowledge of selection commands and how to modify selections.
4.5f	Identify that blending determines how the pixels on a layer interact with the pixels on the layers below.
4.5h	Demonstrate knowledge of opacity and fill.
4.5i	Demonstrate knowledge of when to use various blending mode options.

Filling selections with colors

Explanation

As you create and modify images and artwork, you can apply color to selected image areas. To specify a color, you can use the Color panel, the Swatches panel, the Color Picker dialog box, or the Eyedropper tool.

The Swatches panel

If you're using the same colors repeatedly, you should save them as swatches in the Swatches panel so you won't need to redefine or resample them each time you want to use them. The Swatches panel displays a set of *swatches* (colors) as small color squares by default. You can select a different set of swatches—such as Pantone colors or Web-safe colors—from the Swatches panel menu. In addition, you can customize the Swatches panel by adding your own colors. You can also change how the swatches are displayed in the panel. For example, you can choose Small List from the Swatches panel menu to display the swatches with their names as a list, as shown in Exhibit 1-1.

To add a color to the Swatches panel:

1 Specify the foreground color by using the Color panel, the Eyedropper tool, or the Color Picker dialog box.

2 Add the color to the Swatches panel by using either of these techniques:

- Point to an empty area at the bottom of the Swatches panel, so the pointer appears as a paint bucket, and click to add the color. In the Color Swatch Name dialog box that appears, enter a name and click OK.

- Click the "Create new swatch of foreground color" button. Double-click the new swatch to open the Color Swatch Name dialog box. Enter a name and click OK. (You can also press Alt as you click the "Create new swatch of foreground color" button to open the dialog box.)

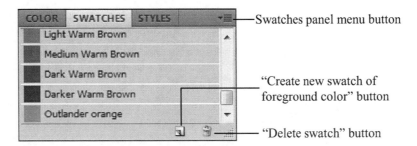

Exhibit 1-1: The Swatches panel in Small List view

If you want to remove a swatch from the Swatches panel, drag the swatch to the Delete swatch icon, or press Alt and click the swatch.

HSB color

You can use the Color panel to specify colors by using a variety of color models, such as RGB, CMYK, or grayscale. Some people prefer to define color by using the *HSB* (hue, saturation, brightness) color model, which many find to be more intuitive. The HSB color model's range is similar to RGB's, but HSB defines colors based on their hue, saturation, and brightness, as shown in Exhibit 1-2.

The hue value is measured in degrees, based on the concept of all available hues being displayed on a circle known as a color wheel. Each degree in the circle represents a different hue along a spectrum. The saturation and brightness values are measured in percentages.

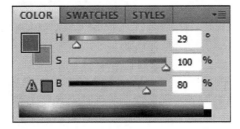

Exhibit 1-2: The Color panel displaying the HSB color sliders

Do it!

A-1: Creating swatches

The files for this activity are in Student Data folder **Unit 1\Topic A**.

Here's how	Here's why
1 Start Adobe Photoshop CS5	
2 Open Outlander logo 1	
Save the image as **My Outlander logo 1**	In the current topic folder.
3 Zoom in on the first **S** in "Spices"	Press and hold Ctrl+Spacebar to access the Zoom tool, and drag across the "S."
Select the Eyedropper tool	
Click the **S**	To sample the orange color as the new foreground color.
4 Click the **Swatches** panel	
Point to the blank area just to the right of the last swatch, as shown	The pointer changes to a paint can.
Click the mouse button	To add the foreground color as a swatch. The Color Swatch Name dialog box appears.
Edit the Name box to read **Outlander orange**	
Click **OK**	To add the orange color to the Swatches panel.
5 In the Swatches panel, click as shown	To display the Swatches panel menu.
Choose **Small List**	To display the swatches as a list.
Scroll to the bottom of the list	To view the Outlander orange swatch.

6 Drag the Swatches panel tab to the left	To separate the panel from its panel group so you can see the Swatches and Color panels at the same time.
Drag the Swatches panel next to the Color panel group, as shown	

7 From the Color panel menu, choose **HSB Sliders**	To display the HSB color model's sliders. You'll use this color model to specify a slightly dimmer version of the color.
Drag the B (Brightness) slider to **80**	To specify a dimmer color.
In the Swatches panel, click ▣	(The "Create new swatch of foreground color" button.) To add the adjusted color as a new swatch. By default, it's named Swatch 1.
8 Double-click **Swatch 1**	To select the swatch name.
Type **Darker orange** and press (↵ ENTER)	To rename the swatch. Next, you'll create a lighter version of the color.
9 In the Color panel, drag the B slider to **100**	
Drag the S (Saturation) slider to **60**	To create a pale orange.
Press and hold (ALT) and click ▣ in the Swatches panel	To add the swatch and automatically open the Color Swatch Name dialog box.
Edit the Name box to read **Lighter orange**	
Click **OK**	
10 Create a color named **Very light orange**, with a Saturation value of **40**	In the Color panel, drag the S slider to 40. In the Swatches panel, Alt+click the "Create new swatch of foreground color" button. Enter "Very light orange" and click OK.

11	In the Swatches panel, click **Darker orange**	To select it as the foreground color
	Press ⟨CTRL⟩ and click **Outlander orange**	To select it as the background color.
	Press ⟨ALT⟩ and click **Very light orange**	To delete the swatch.
12	Dock the Swatches panel	Drag it to the Color panel group.
	Close the image	

Fill shortcuts

Explanation   After you set a color as the foreground or background color, you can apply it by using a variety of techniques.

- To fill a selection on the Background layer with the background color, press Backspace or Delete. (On other layers, pressing Backspace or Delete removes pixels, creating empty areas.)
- To fill a selection with the foreground color, press Alt+Backspace or Alt+Delete.
- To fill a selection with the background color, press Ctrl+Backspace or Ctrl+Delete.
- To apply a fill with custom settings, choose Edit, Fill or press Shift+Backspace to open the Fill dialog box. From the Use list, select Foreground Color or Background Color, or select Color to open the Color Picker, from which you can select any color to use as the new fill. Under Blending, select a mode and specify the opacity for the color you're applying, as shown in Exhibit 1-3.

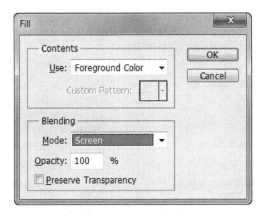

Exhibit 1-3: The Fill dialog box

When you use the Fill dialog box to specify a blending mode for the fill you're applying, the blending mode influences how the new fill affects the existing colors on the current layer. The blending mode won't affect how the new fill interacts with colors on other layers.

File presets

When you choose File, New to create a Photoshop file, you can specify the image's dimensions, resolution, color mode, and background color. Rather than specifying each value manually, you can select an option from the Preset list to specify a standard size or other preset. The following table lists a few of the presets available.

Preset	Specifications
Clipboard	Uses the dimensions and resolution of the item currently on the Clipboard. This is useful when you've cut or copied content that you want to paste into a new Photoshop file.
Default Photoshop Size	7" × 5" at 72ppi.
U.S. Paper	8.5" × 11" at 300 ppi.
Photo	3" × 2" at 300 ppi.
Web	640 pixels × 480 pixels at 72 ppi.
Mobile & Devices	176 pixels × 208 pixels at 72 ppi.
Film & Video	720 pixels × 480 pixels at 72 ppi, with a pixel aspect ratio of 0.91. This matches the frame size of the NTSC video traditionally used for TV broadcasts in the United States. (There's also a widescreen setting with a pixel aspect ratio of 1.21.)
	Unlike computer monitors, which display square pixels, televisions display pixels that are narrower than they are tall. If you view a 720px × 480px image on a computer monitor with square pixels, the image looks wider than it would on TV. When you specify a pixel aspect ratio of 0.91 to match that of TV, Photoshop displays the image within the space of 648 × 480 pixels, approximating its appearance on TV.
	You can change the pixel aspect ratio of any image by using the View, Pixel Aspect Ratio submenu, and turn the correction on or off with the View, Pixel Aspect Ratio Correction command.
<open image name>	Any open images are listed at the bottom of the Preset list. You can select an image name to use its settings for the new image.

Do it!

A-2: Filling selections

Here's how	Here's why
1 Choose **File, New...**	To open the New dialog box.
Edit the Name box to read **My background 1**	
2 From the Preset list, select **Default Photoshop Size**	If necessary.
3 From the Width list, select **pixels**	

Width:	504	pixels ▼
Height:	360	pixels ▼

(If necessary.) To set both the width and the height to pixels.

Edit the Width box to read **600**	
Edit the Height box to read **600**	
Edit the Resolution box to read **300**	

Width:	600	pixels ▼
Height:	600	pixels ▼
Resolution:	300	pixels/inch ▼

4 Observe the Preset value	Because you specified custom settings, the Preset value automatically changed to "Custom."
Click **OK**	To create the new image.
5 Press ⌨CTRL + ⌨A	To select all pixels on the Background layer.
Press ⌨CTRL + ⌨← BACKSPACE	To fill the image with the current background color.
6 Create a layer called **Circles**	Press Alt and click the "Create a new layer" button in the Layers panel. Enter "Circles" in the Name box, and click OK.
Deselect the current selection	Press Ctrl+D.
Create a selection in the shape of a circle	

Use the Elliptical Marquee tool while pressing Shift to create a perfect circle.

7 In the Swatches panel, click **Lighter orange**

To set the foreground color to Lighter orange.

Press (ALT) + (← BACKSPACE)

To fill the selection marquee with the Lighter orange color.

Deselect the current selection

Press Ctrl+D.

8 Make a smaller circular selection inside the first circle, as shown

Press (← BACKSPACE)

To delete the pixels from the Circles layer. Pressing Backspace removes the pixels and creates a transparent area within the selection.

Hide, and then show, the Background layer

(In the Layers panel, click the eye icon next to the Background layer.) To view the transparent space.

9 Press (CTRL) and click **Darker orange**

(In the Swatches panel.) To set that color as the background color.

You will use both the Lighter orange and Darker orange colors repeatedly, so you want them to be available in the Tools panel.

10 Select the Circles layer

If necessary.

Press (CTRL) + (← BACKSPACE)

To fill the selection with the background color.

Deselect the current selection

11 On the Circles layer, draw an overlapping circular marquee, as shown

Verify that Lighter orange is the current foreground color

12 Press (SHIFT) + (← BACKSPACE)

To open the Fill dialog box. You'll use a blending mode to create a semi-transparent effect.

From the Use list, select **Foreground Color**

(If necessary.) To select the Lighter orange color.

13 From the Mode list, select **Screen**

To make the fill color lighten the colors it overlaps.

14 Click **OK**

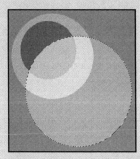

To fill the circle. The blending mode lightened the two circles where the new circle overlaps them. The blending mode had no effect on the orange color in the background, however, because it's on a different layer.

Deselect the current selection

15 Create another circular selection, as shown

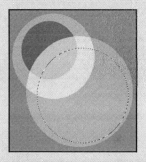

Open the Fill dialog box

Press Shift+Backspace.

From the Mode list, select **Multiply**

Click **OK**

To fill the circle with the foreground color.

16 Deselect the current selection

17 Choose **File**, **Save**

To open the Save As dialog box. The name you specified earlier appears in the File name box.

Navigate to the current topic folder and click **Save**

Fill layers

Explanation

Another way to add a color to an image is to create a *fill layer*. A fill layer can contain a solid color, a gradient, or a pattern.

Applying a fill by using a fill layer requires fewer steps than does creating a blank layer and then filling it. In addition, you might want to use a fill layer to apply a solid color, a gradient, or a pattern because if you later change the image's canvas size, the fill layer will expand to fill the new space.

To create a fill layer:

1 Open the dialog box for the type of fill layer you want to create:

- At the bottom of the Layers panel, click the "Create new fill or adjustment layer" icon and choose Solid Color, Gradient, or Pattern to open the appropriate dialog box.
- Choose Layer, New Fill Layer and choose Solid Color, Gradient, or Pattern to open the New Layer dialog box. Specify the layer name and click OK to open the appropriate dialog box for the type of fill layer you chose.

2 Specify the settings you want.

3 Click OK.

Another benefit of using a fill layer is that you can easily change its settings by double-clicking the fill layer's thumbnail, shown in Exhibit 1-4, to open a dialog box in which you can adjust the color, gradient, or pattern of the fill layer.

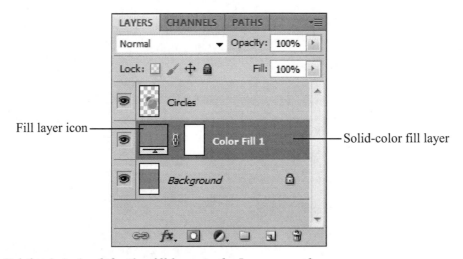

Exhibit 1-4: A solid-color fill layer in the Layers panel

Do it!   **A-3:   Creating fill layers**

Here's how	Here's why
1 Press ⒟	To return the foreground and background colors to their defaults.
2 Choose **Image**, **Canvas Size...**	To open the Canvas Size dialog box. You'll add one inch to the height of the canvas.
Edit the Height box to read **3**	
Verify that Relative is cleared	
In the Canvas extension color list, verify that **Background** is selected	
Click **OK**	The canvas extends an additional inch, but the additional canvas is white (the current background color).
3 Press ⒸⓉⓇⓁ + ⓏΩ	To undo the change. You'll create a fill layer with the background color to see what happens when you resize the canvas.
4 Choose **Layer**, **New Fill Layer**, **Solid Color...**	To open the New Layer dialog box.
Click **OK**	The Color Picker dialog box appears.
In the Swatches panel, click **Outlander orange**	
Click **OK**	
5 Drag the **Color Fill 1** layer below the Circles layer	(In the Layers panel.) You'll add to the canvas size to see the result of the fill layer.
6 Choose **Image**, **Canvas Size...**	To open the Canvas Size dialog box.
Edit the Height box to read **3**	
Click **OK**	The fill layer expands automatically as the canvas expands.
7 Update and close the image	

Topic B: Gradients and patterns

This topic covers the following Adobe ACA exam objectives for Photoshop CS5.

#	Objective
3.1b	Demonstrate knowledge of how to organize and customize the workspace.
3.1c	Demonstrate knowledge of the functions of tools on the Tools panel.
3.2a	Identify and label elements of the different types of layers.
4.4c	Identify advanced adjustment tools and when to use them.
4.5h	Demonstrate knowledge of opacity and fill.

Gradients

Explanation

A *gradient* is a blend of two or more colors, in which the colors fade gradually from one to another. You can use the Gradient tool to drag within a layer or selection to specify the angle and length of a gradient.

The Gradient tool

To create a gradient with the Gradient tool:

1 In the Tools panel, select the Gradient tool.

2 On the options bar, click the Gradient Picker arrow, shown in Exhibit 1-5, to open the Gradient Picker. Select the gradient you want, or choose New Gradient from the Gradient Picker menu to create a custom gradient. Press Esc to close the Gradient Picker.

3 On the options bar, click the icon for the gradient type you want to use, as shown in Exhibit 1-5: Linear, Radial, Angle, Reflected, or Diamond.

The gradient type determines how the colors are arranged. For example, a linear gradient displays colors blending from one to another in a straight line. A radial gradient displays one color at the center and blends outward to the other colors.

4 Drag across the image or selection to specify the angle and length of the gradient.

The distance you drag the Gradient tool specifies the gradient's *blend area:* where the colors blend together. If you drag across only part of the layer or selection, the area outside that region is filled with the gradient's beginning or ending colors.

Gradient Picker arrow

Gradient sample

Exhibit 1-5: Gradient tool settings on the options bar

To modify the gradient's colors and other settings, click the gradient sample on the options bar to open the Gradient Editor dialog box, shown in Exhibit 1-6. To create a new gradient preset, enter a name and click New. Click OK when you're done editing the gradient.

The following table describes some of the settings in the Gradient Editor dialog box.

Setting	Description
Panel menu	Choose a different set of gradients, or change how the gradient list is displayed.
Presets	Click a gradient to view and change its settings. When you do, its name changes to "Custom" so that your changes don't affect the original gradient.
Name box	Enter a name for the gradient.
Color stop	Click a color stop to select it so you can change its color. To move a color stop, drag it or type a position in the Location box. To add a color stop, click below the gradient bar. To remove a color stop, drag it away from the gradient bar. (A gradient must have at least two color stops, so you can't remove the last two.)
Opacity stop	Click an opacity stop to select it so you can change the opacity setting at that location. To move an opacity stop, drag it or type a new position in the Location box. Add an opacity stop by clicking above the gradient bar. Remove a stop by dragging it away from the gradient bar.
Midpoint	When you click a color stop or opacity stop, a diamond appears between it and the next stop. The diamond represents the blending midpoint between the two stops. To adjust the midpoint, drag it or type a new value in the Location box.

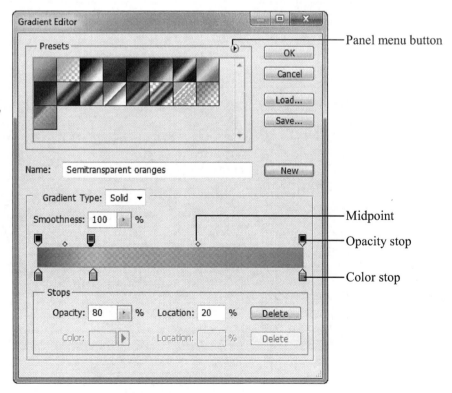

Exhibit 1-6: The Gradient Editor dialog box

Gradient fill layers

You can apply a gradient to an entire layer by creating a gradient fill layer. To create a gradient fill layer:

1 In the Layers panel, click the "Create new fill or adjustment layer" icon and choose Gradient to open the Gradient Fill dialog box.

2 Specify the options you want.

3 Click OK.

To modify the gradient fill layer, double-click its icon in the Layers panel. In the Gradient Fill dialog box, specify the settings you want and click OK.

Gradient Map adjustment

Another way to make use of gradients is to use the Gradient Map adjustment. This adjustment maps the colors of a specified gradient fill to the equivalent shadows, midtones, and highlights in an image. So, for example, if you mapped a three-color gradient fill to an image, one endpoint of the gradient would map to the shadows, the center color stop would map to the midtones, and the other endpoint would map to the highlights in the image. The result isn't a gradient (unless you've manually applied one in the image) but is rather an adjustment layer that replaces image colors.

To use the Gradient Map adjustment, click the Gradient Map icon in the Adjustments panel to create an adjustment layer. Then, in the Adjustment Panel's Gradient Picker, select the desired gradient.

Do it!

B-1: Creating gradients

The files for this activity are in Student Data folder **Unit 1\Topic B**.

Here's how	Here's why
1 Open Background 2	
Save the image as **My background 2**	In the current topic folder.
2 Press (CTRL) + (0)	To fit the image on the screen.
3 Select the Circles layer	(If necessary.) In the Layers panel.
4 Set the foreground color to **Lighter orange**	In the Swatches panel, click Lighter orange.
Set the background color to **Darker orange**	In the Swatches panel, press Ctrl and click Darker orange.
5 Create a layer named **Fade**	
Drag the layer below the Circles layer	

6 In the Tools panel, click   The Gradient tool.

   Display the Gradient Picker   Click the Gradient Picker arrow on the options bar.

   In the Gradient Picker, verify that the first gradient is selected, as shown

   The Foreground to Background gradient.

   Press (ESC)   To close the Gradient Picker.

7 Drag from the top-left corner of the image to the bottom-right corner   To create the gradient.

8 Observe the image   The gradient goes from the top-left corner to the bottom-right corner.

   Next, you'll create a gradient and apply it to another layer.

9 On the options bar, click the gradient sample

   To open the Gradient Editor dialog box. You'll create a gradient that includes three colors.

   Click the left color stop, as shown

   To select the foreground color stop.

10 In the Swatches panel, click **Darker orange**   To apply the color as the foreground color of the gradient.

   Click the right color stop, as shown

   To select the background color stop.

   Set the color to **Outlander orange**   In the Swatches panel, click Outlander orange.

11 Click below the gradient bar, as shown

To create another color stop.

Set the color for the new stop to **Lighter orange**

Drag the color midpoint diamonds closer to the center color stop, as shown

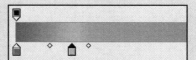

To make the Lighter orange portion of the gradient narrower.

Next, you'll lower the opacity for the gradient at the center stop.

12 Click above the gradient bar, as shown

To create an opacity stop above the center color stop.

Under Stops, edit the Opacity value to read **80**

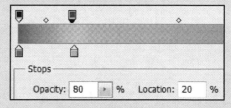

To create a slightly transparent area of the gradient.

13 Edit the Name box to read **Semitransparent oranges**

Click **New**

To save the custom gradient.

Click **OK**

To close the dialog box.

14 Above the Circles layer, create a layer named **Highlight**

15 In the Highlight layer, use the **Semitransparent oranges** gradient to create a linear gradient extending from the top-right corner of the image to the bottom-left corner

Drag from the top-right corner to the bottom-left corner. Because the new gradient is semitransparent, you can see through it to the circles you created on the layer below.

16 Update the image

Patterns

Explanation

In addition to using solid colors and gradients, you can fill a layer or selection with a pattern. A *pattern* is a rectangular image area that repeats to fill a layer or selection. You can apply one of Photoshop's default patterns, or create your own.

To create a custom pattern:

1   Use the Rectangular Marquee tool to select the image area you want to define as a pattern. The selection must use a Feather value of zero.
2   Choose Edit, Define Pattern to open the Pattern Name dialog box.
3   In the Name box, enter a name for the pattern.
4   Click OK.

To apply a pattern to a layer or an image area:

1   In the Layers panel, click the layer you want to fill with the pattern, or use a selection tool to select the area you want to fill. If there is no selection, the pattern will fill the entire layer.
2   Press Shift+Backspace or choose Edit, Fill to open the Fill dialog box.
3   From the Use list, select Pattern.
4   From the Custom Pattern list, select the pattern you want to use. You can use the Custom Pattern panel menu to change how the patterns are displayed in the list or to select a different set of patterns.
5   Under Blending, specify any blending options you want to use.
6   Click OK.

Offset patterns

Instead of creating a pattern in which a repeating item appears in columns and rows, you can create an offset pattern, as shown in Exhibit 1-7.

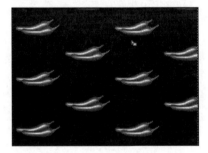

Exhibit 1-7: An offset pattern

To create an offset pattern:

1 Create a pattern using the item that you want to display as an offset pattern.

2 Create a new image that is twice the height and width of a single tile of the pattern you created.

3 Fill the image with the pattern, which will tile four times in the image—two vertical tiles and two horizontal tiles.

4 Make a selection that includes two vertical tiles of the pattern (the entire image height and half its width).

5 Choose Filter, Other, Offset. Specify a vertical offset value that is half the height of a single pattern tile, and click OK. The two tiles you selected and offset are now offset from the other two tiles in the image.

6 Select the entire image, and create a new pattern. When you fill an image with the new pattern, it will appear as an offset pattern, as shown in Exhibit 1-7.

Pattern fill layers

You can also add a pattern to an image by using a pattern fill layer. To create a pattern fill layer:

1 In the Layers panel, click the "Create new fill or adjustment layer" icon and choose Pattern to open the Pattern Fill dialog box.

2 Specify the options you want.

3 Click OK.

If you want to modify the pattern fill layer, double-click its icon to open the Pattern Fill dialog box. Specify settings and click OK.

Do it!

B-2: Creating a simple pattern

The files for this activity are in Student Data folder **Unit 1\Topic B**.

Here's how	Here's why
1 Open Outlander logo 2	
Choose **View**, **Fit on Screen**	If necessary, to display the entire image.
2 Select the Rectangular Marquee tool	
On the options bar, from the Style list, select **Fixed Size**	
Edit the Width box to read **160 px**	
Edit the Height box to read **160 px**	To set the marquee to a fixed size and a square shape.

3 Click in the image

To place the marquee. Because the marquee was set to a fixed size, you didn't need to drag to create it.

Drag the marquee to position it as shown

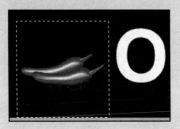

4 Choose **Edit**,
   Define Pattern...

To open the Pattern Name dialog box.

Edit the Name box to read **Chiles**

Click **OK**

To create the pattern.

5 Switch to the My background 2 image

Click the image's tab.

Below the Circles layer, create a layer named **Chiles**

6 Press (SHIFT) + (← BACKSPACE)

To open the Fill dialog box.

From the Use list, select **Pattern**

From the Custom Pattern list, select the **Chiles** pattern

Press Esc to close the Custom Pattern list.

From the Mode list, select **Normal**

Click **OK**

To fill the layer with the Chiles pattern.

7 Update and close
   My background 2

Close Outlander Logo 2 without updating the image

The Preset Manager

Explanation

Each swatch, gradient, or pattern—both those you create and those supplied with Photoshop—is called a *preset*. Brushes, styles, contours, custom shapes, and tool settings are also stored as presets.

You can use the Preset Manager dialog box to load presets that come with Photoshop. You can also use the Preset Manager dialog box to save a group of presets you've created or edited. The group is saved as a file called a *set*. Sets can be useful for a few reasons:

- You can share sets of presets with other people for consistency.

- You can create multiple preset files that you can load for different purposes (for example, a designer could save different color panels for different clients).

- If you need to reinstall Photoshop, you can reload the presets you saved instead of losing them.

To manage presets and sets:

1 Choose Edit, Preset Manager (or choose Preset Manager from a panel menu).

2 From the Preset Type list, select one of the eight preset types.

3 Select the presets you want to work with. Shift+click to select a range of adjacent presets, or Ctrl+click to select non-adjacent ones.

4 Click Save Set to save the selected presets as a set. If you save the set in the default location (a subfolder of the Presets folder within the Photoshop application folder), then after you close and re-open Photoshop, the set will appear in the panel menu, along with sets that came with Photoshop.

5 Select options from the Preset Manager list to change the display, to reset or replace presets, or to select a set from the ones listed.

Do it!

B-3: Saving a set of presets

Here's how	Here's why
1 Choose **Edit**, **Preset Manager...**	To open the Preset Manager dialog box. You'll save, as a set, the three colors you added to the Swatches panel earlier.
2 From the Preset Type list, select **Swatches**	
3 Click the Outlander orange swatch (the third from the last)	
Press (SHIFT) and click the last swatch	To select the range of three adjacent swatches you created.
4 Click **Save Set**	To open the Save dialog box.
Edit the File name box to read **Outlander oranges**	
In the Save in list, verify that the **Color Swatches** folder is selected	To ensure that the set will be saved alongside the swatch sets that came with Photoshop.
Click **Save**	To save the set. You can now delete these swatches and reload them later if necessary.
5 Click **Delete**	To delete the swatches you created.
Click **Done**	The swatches are removed from the Swatches panel. To make the Outlander oranges set appear in the panel menu, you need to close and re-open Photoshop.
6 Close Photoshop	
Start Photoshop	
7 From the Swatches panel menu, choose **Outlander oranges**	A warning box appears, asking whether you want to replace the current swatches or append the new set.
Click **Append**	To add the colors to the existing ones.
8 In the Swatches panel, scroll down	To see that the set of Outlander oranges colors has been added to the swatches.

Tool presets

Explanation

A tool preset is one of the eight categories of presets. You can use tool presets to save and reuse specified settings for a particular tool.

To create a tool preset:

1 Select the tool for which you want to create a preset.
2 On the options bar, specify the tool settings you want to store as a preset.
3 Do either of the following to open the New Tool Preset dialog box:

- On the left side of the options bar, click the Tool Preset icon to display the Tool Preset picker, and click the "Create new tool preset" button.
- Choose Window, Tool Presets to open the Tool Presets panel, and click the "Create new tool preset" button.

4 In the New Tool Preset dialog box, enter a name for the preset and click OK.

After saving a tool preset, you can select it from the Tool Preset picker or from the Tool Presets panel. If you want to reset the current tool to its default settings, then right-click the Tool Preset icon on the options bar and choose Reset Tool.

Do it!

B-4: Creating a tool preset

The files for this activity are in Student Data folder **Unit 1\Topic B**.

Here's how	Here's why
1 Select the Rectangular Marquee tool	(If necessary.) You'll create two presets for this tool, representing two sets of selection marquee dimensions that you'll use often in your work.
2 In the Style list, verify that **Fixed Size** is selected Edit the Width and Height boxes to read **90 px**	(On the options bar.) You'll create a preset that creates 90-pixel square selections.
3 Click as shown to display the Tool Preset picker	
Click the "Create new tool preset" button, as shown	 To open the New Tool Preset dialog box.
4 Edit the Name box to read **Rectangular 90 px** Click **OK**	To save the tool preset. The options bar displays the settings you specified.

5 Edit the Width box to read **45 px**   On the options bar.

Edit the Feather box to read **5 px**

Save the current settings as a   (Display the Tool Preset picker and click the
preset named   "Create new tool preset" button. Enter the new
Rectangular 45x90 px,   preset's name and click OK.) You can now
5 px Feather   switch among these two presets.

6 Choose **Window**,   To open the Tool Presets panel.
Tool Presets

Observe the list of presets in the   The two tool presets you just created appear in
panel   the panel.

7 Click the **Rectangular 90 px**   (In the Tool Presets panel.) To select the preset.
preset

Observe the options bar settings   The options bar displays the preset's settings.

8 Open Background 2

Click within the image   To generate a selection based on the current
settings.

Press ⌈CTRL⌉ + ⌈D⌉

9 Click the **Rectangular 45x90**   (In the Tool Presets panel.) To select the preset.
px, 5 px Feather preset   The options bar displays this preset's settings.

Click within the image   To generate a selection based on this preset's
settings.

Press ⌈CTRL⌉ + ⌈D⌉

10 Close the Tool Presets panel   You'll return the Rectangular Marquee tool to
its default settings.

11 On the options bar, right-click as
shown

To display a shortcut menu.

Choose **Reset Tool**   To return the Rectangular Marquee tool settings
on the options bar to the defaults. The tool
presets you created are still available.

12 Close Background 2

Topic C: Layer overlays

This topic covers the following Adobe ACA exam objectives for Photoshop CS5.

#	Objective
4.8b	Demonstrate knowledge of how to apply and remove layer effects or layer styles.
4.8c	Demonstrate knowledge of how to apply layer styles to type.

Overlay layer styles

Explanation

Another way to apply a fill, gradient, or pattern to a layer is to use an overlay layer style. An *overlay layer style* applies a fill, gradient, or pattern to only the existing pixels in a layer, similar to creating a layer clipping mask.

Gradient overlays

The Gradient Overlay layer style fills the existing layer content with the gradient you specify. This layer style is particularly useful for applying a gradient to text; even after applying a gradient overlay, you can continue to edit and format the text.

By default, a gradient overlay aligns with the layer content. Therefore, if you change the text on a type layer, or paint additional areas on a layer, the gradient adjusts automatically to flow across the new layer content.

To specify settings for the gradient overlay, select Gradient Overlay from the list of styles in the Layer Style dialog box. The Gradient Overlay style options are shown in Exhibit 1-8.

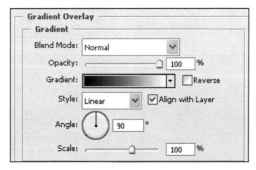

Exhibit 1-8: The Gradient Overlay options in the Layer Style dialog box

To create an overlay layer style:

1   Double-click the layer thumbnail or the space to the right of the layer name to open the Layer Style dialog box.

2   In the list of styles, select the type of overlay you want to use: Color Overlay, Gradient Overlay, or Pattern Overlay.

3   Specify the options you want to use, such as transparency.

4   For gradient and pattern overlays, point to the image and drag to reposition the gradient or pattern relative to the layer content through which it appears. This technique works only while the Layer Style dialog box is open.

5   Click OK.

Do it!

C-1:   Filling areas with overlay layer styles

The files for this activity are in Student Data folder **Unit 1\Topic C**.

Here's how	Here's why
1 Open Background 3	
Save the image as **My background 3**	In the current topic folder.
2 Double-click the Chiles layer thumbnail	To open the Layer Style dialog box. You'll dim the chiles to make the pattern more subdued.
3 Under Styles, click **Color Overlay**	(Click the words themselves, not the checkbox to their left). To check the checkbox and display the Color Overlay settings.
Click the color swatch next to the Blend Mode list, as shown	*Blend Mode: Normal* ▼ *Opacity:* ――――― 100 % To open the Select overlay color dialog box.
Click as shown	To specify a black color.
  ○ R: 0 ○ G: 0 ○ B: 0 ☐ Only Web Colors # 000000	
Click **OK**	To select the black color for the overlay.
4 Set the Opacity value to **50%**	
Click **OK**	To overlay the layer with a semi-transparent black color, dimming it slightly.
5 Select the Horizontal Type tool	You'll add some text.
Set the font to **Impact** and the size to **30 pt**	
Set the foreground and background colors to the defaults	Press D.
6 Select the Highlight layer	You want the type layer to appear on top.
Click to place the insertion point near the left edge of the image	
Type **Hot stuff!**	To create a type layer.
Using the Move tool, center the text horizontally and vertically	

7 In the Layers panel, double-click the Hot Stuff! layer

To open the Layer Style dialog box.

8 Click **Gradient Overlay**

To display the Gradient Overlay settings.

From the Gradient list, select **Violet, Orange** as indicated

Check **Reverse**

To reverse the gradient colors.

Clear **Align with Layer**

Click **OK**

To apply the gradient overlay to the type layer.

9 Using the Move tool, drag the text to the top of the image

The colors in the text change as you move it. This occurs because the gradient applies to the whole image.

10 In the Hot Stuff! layer, double-click the **Gradient Overlay** layer effect name

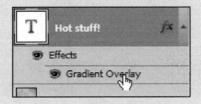

To open the Layer Style dialog box.

Check **Align with Layer**

11 Move the Layer Style dialog box

If necessary, to see the type layer in the image. You'll adjust the gradient's alignment in the layer.

Click in the image and drag down

To adjust the gradient overlay.

Click **OK**

To close the dialog box.

12 Using the Move tool, drag the text up and down within the image

The gradient remains aligned with the type layer as you move it.

13 Update and close the image

Unit summary: Fills and overlays

Topic A   In this topic, you added colors to the **Swatches panel**, and you used fill shortcuts to fill selections and layers with color. In addition, you used **fill layers** to create layers filled with solid color.

Topic B   In this topic, you learned how to use the Gradient tool to add a **gradient** to a layer or selection. You also learned how to create a **gradient fill layer** to add a gradient to an image. Next, you created and applied a fill by using **patterns**. Finally, you used the Preset Manager to save a set of color swatches as a **preset** and to save tool presets.

Topic C   In this topic, you learned how to use **overlay layer styles** to fill layer content with a color, gradient, or pattern.

Independent practice activity

In this activity, you'll create custom swatches and save them as a set. You'll also apply fills, create a pattern, and create an offset pattern. Finally, you'll create a fill layer and apply an overlay layer style.

The files for this activity are in Student Data folder **Unit 1\Unit summary**.

1   Open Practice logo and save the image as **My practice logo**.

2   Create three swatches by sampling colors from the chile pepper. Sample a dark red color, a light red color, and a dark green color, and name the new colors **Chile dark red**, **Chile light red**, and **Chile dark green**.

3   Save the three colors as a swatch preset set named **Chile colors**.

4   Create an image named **Triangles** that's 5"×5" at 300ppi, in RGB color mode.

5   Set the foreground color to Chile dark red, and set the background color to Chile dark green.

6   On a blank new layer, create a triangular selection with the Polygonal Lasso tool, as shown in Exhibit 1-9. Fill the selection with the foreground color. Create another triangle that overlaps the first one, and fill it with the background color, using the Multiply blending mode. (*Hint:* To make horizontal or vertical lines with the Polygonal Lasso, click Shift while selecting points. Use the Fill dialog box to apply a blending mode to a fill.)

7   Close Triangles. (Or if you have time, create additional overlapping triangular selections, filling them with the colors you defined and using blending modes to create a geometric design.)

8   Create a simple pattern, using the word "Outlander" from the My practice logo image. Make the dimension of the tiles 600 pixels wide by 160 pixels tall.

9   Create an image named **Logo bg** that's 600×600 pixels at 300ppi and uses RGB color mode.

10 Create a layer, and fill it with the background color (Chile dark green).

11 Fill the image with the Outlander logo pattern you created, using a Pattern Overlay layer style at 20% opacity. In addition, use the Lighten blend mode and apply a 25% scale. (*Hint:* Double-click the space to the right of the layer name to open the Layer Style dialog box.)

12 Save and close all images.

Exhibit 1-9: The two triangles as they appear after Step 6

Review questions

1 True or false? In the Swatches panel, a swatch can consist of a color, pattern, or gradient.

2 Which key do you press with Alt, Ctrl, or Shift to form shortcuts for filling image areas or opening the Fill dialog box?

3 To fill an image with color that automatically expands if you enlarge the canvas size, what should you create?

4 After specifying tool settings on the options bar, how can you save those settings as a tool preset? [Choose all that apply.]

A On the options bar, right-click the Tool Preset icon and choose Reset Tool.

B Click the Tool Preset icon to display the Tool Preset picker, and click the "Create new tool preset" button.

C Choose Window, Tool Presets to open the Tool Presets panel, and click the "Create new tool preset" button.

D Select an option from the list of presets in the Tool Preset picker.

5 You want to add a gradient on the current layer. Which technique should you use?

    A Choose Layer, New Fill Layer, Gradient.

    B In the Layers panel, click the "Create new fill or adjustment layer" icon and choose Gradient.

    C Select the Gradient tool, select a gradient from the Gradient Picker, and drag in the image.

    D Select a gradient swatch in the Swatches panel and then press Alt+Delete to fill the layer with that gradient.

6 Which of the following statements is true about the selected area you use to define a pattern?

    A The selection must be perfectly square.

    B The selection must be rectangular.

    C The selection can be any shape.

    D The selection can have any feather value.

7 You've added several colors to the Swatches panel. Which command can you use to save them as a set that you can load at any time or share with others?

    A Edit, Preset Manager

    B Select, Save Selection

    C Layer, New Fill Layer, Solid Color

    D Image, Adjustments, Replace Color

8 For what purposes might you use the Preset Manager dialog box? [Choose all that apply.]

    A To reset all Photoshop preferences.

    B To save the current panel locations so you can return to that panel arrangement at any time.

    C To load a set of brushes for use with the Brush tool.

    D To export a set of custom tool presets as a file so you can load the tool presets on a coworker's computer.

9 To create a gradient that automatically aligns with a type layer's contents even when you edit the text, what should you use?

10 What dialog box do overlays appear in?

Unit 2

Masks

Unit time: 50 minutes

Complete this unit, and you'll know how to:

A Paint in Quick Mask mode and in an alpha channel to specify a selection.

B Create a layer mask to hide part of a layer.

C Create grayscale masks to partially mask part of an image.

D Use a clipping mask to conform one layer to the shape of another.

Topic A: Mask channels

This topic covers the following Adobe ACA exam objectives for Photoshop CS5.

#	Objective
3.2b	Demonstrate knowledge of masks and modes.
3.2c	Demonstrate knowledge of how to create masks.
4.1b	Demonstrate knowledge of saving, loading, and editing selections.

Using masks

Explanation

When you select part of an image, the areas outside the selection are *masked*, because you can't paint in those areas. This concept is similar to a painter using masking tape to cover areas that should not be painted.

In addition to using Photoshop's selection tools to select image areas, you can use painting tools to select areas. The painting tools can be more intuitive than the selection tools and can make it easier to add to or subtract from a complex selection. To specify image selections by painting, you can paint in Quick Mask mode or in an alpha channel.

Quick Masks

One way to create a selection by painting is to use *Quick Mask mode*. This mode displays a semi-transparent colored overlay to differentiate between selected and non-selected areas. By default, the color appears over all areas of the image that are not selected (the masked areas), although you can reverse this. In Quick Mask mode, you can use the painting tools to add to or subtract from the selection. In its default configuration, painting with black adds to the masked area, and painting with white adds to the selected area.

To activate Quick Mask mode, click the Edit in Quick Mask Mode button in the Tools panel or press Q. To return to Standard mode (in which a selection appears as a marquee), click the Edit in Standard Mode button or press Q.

By default, the masking color is red. If that's difficult to distinguish from the image itself, you can change the masking color.

To change the masking color:

1 Double-click the Edit in Quick Mask Mode button to open the Quick Mask Options dialog box, shown in Exhibit 2-1.
2 Click the color swatch to open the Select Quick Mask Color dialog box.
3 Specify the color you want to use, and click OK.
4 Under Color, adjust the Opacity value, if necessary.
5 Click OK.

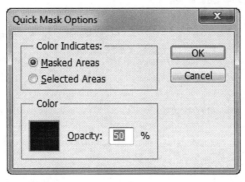

Exhibit 2-1: The Quick Mask Options dialog box

Do it!

A-1:   Editing a Quick Mask

The files for this activity are in Student Data folder **Unit 2\Topic A**.

Here's how	Here's why
1 Open Puppy 1	
Save the image as **My puppy 1**	You'll use the Magnetic Lasso tool to select the puppy, and then you'll clean up the selection by painting in Quick Mask mode.
2 Select the Magnetic Lasso tool	
3 Very quickly, draw a selection marquee around the puppy, as shown	
	(Click where you want to begin the selection, and then move the pointer around the dog *without* holding down the mouse button.) Don't add points to get an extremely accurate selection; you'll clean up the selection in Quick Mask mode.
4 At the bottom of the Tools panel, click as shown	
	(The Edit in Quick Mask Mode button.) To enter Quick Mask mode. The unselected areas of the image appear as transparent red. The red color is difficult to see against the brown background, so you'll change the mask color to blue.
5 In the Tools panel, double-click	To open the Quick Mask Options dialog box.
Click the color swatch	To open the Select Quick Mask Color dialog box.
Edit the R box to read **0**	
Edit the B box to read **255**	
Click **OK** twice	To return to the image.

6 Click 🔘	To return to Quick Mask mode. The blue color makes it easier to see the masked areas of the image. You'll now paint in Quick Mask mode to fine-tune the selection.
7 Press Ⓓ	To set the foreground and background colors to their defaults.
8 Select the Brush tool	
Open the Brush Preset picker	On the options bar.
Specify a Size setting of **9 px**	
Specify a Hardness setting of **100%**	
Click the Brush Preset picker	To close it.
9 Paint any areas that should be masked	(That is, paint those areas around the puppy that should *not* be part of the selection.) Painting with black adds to the masked area.
10 Press Ⓧ	To switch the foreground and background colors. Painting with white subtracts from the masked area.
Paint the areas of the dog that should be visible but are masked with blue	
11 As necessary, press Ⓧ to switch the foreground and background colors as you touch up the mask	Zoom in as necessary.
12 Update the image	

Alpha channel masks

Explanation

Another way that you can paint a masked area to add to or subtract from a selection is to paint in an *alpha channel* (an additional channel that doesn't contribute to the image itself, as color channels do). When you save a selection as an alpha channel, the alpha channel is created as an area of black and white pixels, with black representing masked areas, and white representing selected areas. Gray areas in an alpha channel represent semi-selected areas, such as a feathered area.

To paint in an alpha channel to modify a saved selection:

1 In the Channels panel, click the alpha channel to display it in the image window. You can view the channel as a Quick Mask overlay over the image by showing the composite channel at the top of the Channels panel.

2 Paint with black to add to the masked area, and paint with white to add to the selected area.

3 Click the channel at the top of the Channels panel to view the image in the image window.

Do it!

A-2: Editing an alpha channel as a Quick Mask

Here's how	Here's why
1 Click 🔲	(At the bottom of the Tools panel.) To enter Standard mode and show the selection marquee.
2 Click the **Channels** panel	
In the Channels panel, click 🔲	(The "Save selection as channel" button.) To save the selection in an alpha channel, which is named Alpha 1 by default.
3 Deselect the selection	Press Ctrl+D.
In the Channels panel, click **Alpha 1**	To display the channel in the image window. The selected areas of the image are white, and the unselected areas are black.
4 In the Channels panel, click the visibility column to the left of the RGB composite channel	To display the Alpha 1 channel as a Quick Mask overlay.
5 To the left of the dog, paint with white	 To add to the selected area.

6 In the Channels panel, click the visibility column to the left of the RGB composite channel

To hide all channels except the Alpha 1 channel.

Observe the Alpha 1 channel in the image window

The area you painted is added to the mask.

7 In the Channels panel, click the **RGB** composite channel

(Click the channel itself, not the visibility column.) To show the image in the image window without the Quick Mask overlay.

8 Press [CTRL] and click the **Alpha 1** channel

To load the Alpha 1 channel as a selection. The selected area now includes the area you just painted.

Deselect the selected area of the image

9 In the Channels panel, click the **Alpha 1** channel

To show the channel in the image window.

Paint with black on the white area you added next to the puppy

(Press X to switch the background and foreground colors.) To remove the extra area that you just painted.

10 In the Channels panel, click the **RGB** composite channel

To show the image in the image window.

11 Update and close the image

Topic B: Layer masks

This topic covers the following Adobe ACA exam objectives for Photoshop CS5.

#	Objective
3.2b	Demonstrate knowledge of masks and modes.
3.2c	Demonstrate knowledge of how to create masks.
3.2f	Demonstrate knowledge of how to flatten layers.

Creating layer masks

Explanation

When you want to show only part of a layer's contents, you can create a *layer mask*. That way, you can change which part of the layer is visible at any time, or you can reveal the entire layer again if necessary.

To create a layer mask, first select the part of the layer that you want to show. The unselected area will be hidden by the layer mask. Then, at the bottom of the Layers panel, click the Add layer mask button. The Layers panel will display a layer thumbnail and a layer mask thumbnail for that layer, as shown in Exhibit 2-2.

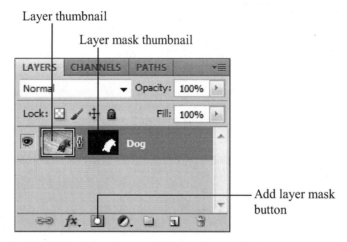

Exhibit 2-2: A layer containing a layer mask

Converting the Background layer

When you create a Photoshop file with a white background, the image contains a single Background layer, which is always the lowest layer in the stacking order. You cannot change the Background layer's blending mode or opacity, nor can you add a layer mask to it. However, because an image doesn't need to include a Background layer, you can convert it to a regular layer. To do so, in the Layers panel, double-click the Background layer to open the New Layer dialog box. Enter a name for the converted layer and click OK.

To convert a regular layer to a Background layer, select it and choose Layer, New, Background from Layer. An image can include only one Background layer. To flatten all layers in an image down to a single Background layer, choose Layer, Flatten Image.

Do it!   **B-1:   Creating a layer mask**

The files for this activity are in Student Data folder **Unit 2\Topic B**.

Here's how	Here's why
1 Open Puppy 2	
Save the image as **My puppy 2**	In the current topic folder.
2 Click the **Layers** panel	You'll use a layer mask to isolate the dog from its background. You can't add a layer mask to the Background layer, though, so you'll convert it to a regular layer.
Double-click the Background layer	To open the New Layer dialog box.
Edit the Name box to read **Dog**	
Click **OK**	
3 Click the **Channels** panel	
Press ⌈CTRL⌋ and click the **Alpha 1** channel	To load the channel as a selection.
4 Click the **Layers** panel	
Click ▨	(The Add layer mask button.) To add a layer mask for the unselected area of the image.
5 Observe the Dog layer in the Layers panel	
	The Dog layer now has a layer thumbnail and a layer mask thumbnail. Next, you'll add a solid white background to the image.
6 In the Layers panel, click ▨	(The "Create new fill or adjustment layer" button.) To display a pop-up menu.
Choose **Solid Color...**	To create a solid-color fill layer. The "Pick a solid color" dialog box appears.
Select a white color	In either the dialog box or the Swatches panel.
Click **OK**	To close the dialog box.
7 In the Layers panel, drag the new layer below the Dog layer	Now the dog appears over a white background.
8 Update the image	

Editing layer masks

Explanation

After applying a layer mask to hide part of a layer, you might want to modify the layer mask. To add to or subtract from a layer mask, activate it by clicking the layer mask thumbnail. Otherwise, you'll be painting over the layer pixels themselves. When you activate the layer mask, the image's appearance in the image window doesn't change. However, when you paint with black in the image, you add to the mask (subtracting from the selection), and when you paint with white, you add to the selection.

If you want to return to editing the image itself, click the image thumbnail in the Layers panel. In addition, you can use the following techniques to change your view of the layer mask thumbnail:

- To view the layer mask in the image window, press Alt and click the layer mask thumbnail.
- To view the image in the image window, click the layer thumbnail or press Alt and click the layer mask thumbnail.
- To disable the layer mask, revealing the entire layer, press Shift and click the layer mask thumbnail.
- To enable the layer mask, hiding the masked areas, press Shift and click the layer mask thumbnail again.

You can change many layer mask options by using the Masks panel, shown in Exhibit 2-3.

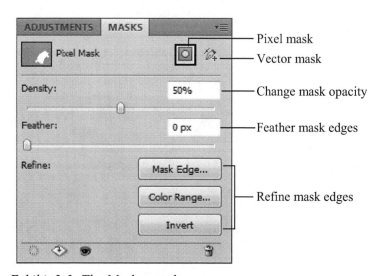

Exhibit 2-3: The Masks panel

Do it!

B-2:   Editing a layer mask

Here's how	Here's why
1 Click the layer mask thumbnail for the Dog layer	(If necessary.) To activate the mask.
2 Paint with black on the areas outside the puppy that you want to add to the mask	To clean up the selection.
Press ⓧ	To switch the background and foreground colors.
Paint with white any areas of the puppy that you want to add to the selection	If necessary.
3 Choose **View, Fit on Screen**	If necessary.
4 Press (ALT) and click the layer mask thumbnail	To view the mask.
Click the layer thumbnail	To return to viewing the image.
5 Press (SHIFT) and click the layer mask thumbnail	
	To disable the layer mask. A red "X" appears over the layer mask thumbnail, and the entire layer is visible.
Press (SHIFT) and click the layer mask thumbnail again	To re-enable the layer mask.
6 In the Layers panel, select the Dog layer	You'll change the opacity of the mask.
7 Show the **Masks** panel	
Click ▣	(The Pixel Mask button.) To activate the mask.
Drag the Density slider to **50%**	To lower the opacity of the mask.
Drag the Density slider to **100%**	To return the mask to normal opacity.
8 Update and close the image	

Topic C: Grayscale masks

This topic covers the following Adobe ACA exam objectives for Photoshop CS5.

#	Objective
3.2b	Demonstrate knowledge of masks and modes.
3.2c	Demonstrate knowledge of how to create masks.

Softening mask edges

Explanation

You can paint with white and black in a mask to add to and subtract from a selection. However, you might want to create a layer mask that has soft or feathered edges. To specify a soft or feathered edge in a mask, apply a gray color. In a mask, shades of gray represent regions that are partially masked. Partially masked areas appear semi-transparent. The darker the gray color, the more transparent the layer contents will be through the mask.

To specify soft or feathered edges in a mask, you can use several techniques:

- Convert a feathered selection to a mask.
- Paint in the layer mask with a soft-edged brush.
- Apply a blur filter to the layer mask.
- Use the Masks panel to feather the mask.

Do it!

C-1:   Creating soft edges with a grayscale mask

The files for this activity are in Student Data folder **Unit 2\Topic C**.

Here's how	Here's why
1 Open Puppy 3	
Save the image as **My puppy 3**	(In the current topic folder.) For an advertisement, you'll create a soft-edged "thought bubble" containing a chicken dish.
2 Open Chicken	
3 Choose **Window, Arrange, Float in Window**	
Using the Move tool, drag the image from the Chicken window into the My puppy 3 window	To create a new layer in the My puppy 3 image.
Close Chicken	
Drag the chicken image so it snaps to the top-left corner of the My puppy 3 image	
4 Name the new layer **Chicken dish**	

5 Select the Lasso tool

   On the options bar, set the Feather value to **10**

   Draw a cloud shape around the dish, as shown

6 In the Layers panel, add a layer mask to the Chicken dish layer

(Click the Add layer mask icon.) To create a feathered layer mask in the shape of the cloud.

Next, you'll add small clouds below the "thought bubble."

7 Select the Brush tool

   In the Brush Preset picker, specify a brush with Size **45 px** and Hardness **0%**

8 For the Chicken dish layer, verify that the layer mask thumbnail is selected

Not the layer thumbnail.

9 Press (x) as necessary to set the foreground color to white

   Between the dog and the cloud containing the chicken dish, paint two small cloud shapes, as shown

Painting in white on the layer mask removes the mask from the painted area, revealing the layer.

10 Zoom to 100% magnification

The edges of the puppy look too sharp against the white background. You'll create a softer edge for the puppy.

11 Select the Dog layer	You'll use the Masks panel to feather the edge of the mask.
In the Masks panel, click the Pixel Mask button	
Drag the Feather slider to **2 px**	To add a 2-pixel feather. You'll refine the feathered edge.
12 Click **Mask Edge**	To open the Refine Mask dialog box.
Drag the Smooth slider to **25**	
Click **OK**	The dog's fur looks softer and more natural against the white background.
13 Choose **View**, **Fit on Screen**	
14 Select the Chicken dish layer	
Using the Move tool, drag the chicken dish around in the image	Both the layer mask and the underlying layer content move together because they're linked.
Click the chain icon between the layer thumbnail and the layer mask thumbnail, as shown	
	To unlink the layer from the layer mask.
Select the layer thumbnail	If necessary.
Using the Move tool, drag the chicken dish around in the image	The picture moves, while the layer mask stays in place.
15 Reposition the chicken dish as desired within the thought balloon	
In the Chicken dish layer, click between the layer thumbnail and the layer mask thumbnail, as shown	
	To re-link the layer with the layer mask.
Reposition the layer as desired	
16 Update and close the image	

Gradient masks

Explanation

Another way to create a grayscale mask is to apply a gradient to part or all of a layer mask. Applying a gradient to a layer mask is useful when you want layer content to gradually fade across a specific area, rather than just display softened edges. For example, you might want to combine two images, with one fading gradually into the other. To apply a gradient to a layer mask:

1 Create a layer mask.

2 Select the Gradient tool.

3 In the Gradient Picker (on the options bar), select the Black, White gradient.

4 In the Layers panel, verify that the layer mask thumbnail is selected.

5 Drag across the image to specify the area you want to fade.

Do it!

C-2: Fading a layer with a gradient mask

The files for this activity are in Student Data folder **Unit 2\Topic C**.

Here's how	Here's why
1 Open Hawaii 1	
Save the image as **My Hawaii 1**	You'll fade out the right side of the image to the white background, but you'll use a layer mask so you can change it later if you wish.
2 Select the Photo layer	If necessary.
3 Add a layer mask to the layer	Click the Add layer mask button at the bottom of the Layers panel.
Verify that the layer mask thumbnail is selected	
4 Select the Gradient tool	
In the Gradient Picker, select the **Black, White** gradient, as shown	
Verify that the Linear Gradient option is selected	On the options bar.
Check **Reverse**	To reverse the gradient colors so the gradient goes from white to black.
5 Show the document rulers	Choose View, Rulers.
Drag a horizontal gradient from 1.5" to 3.5"	Because the gradient is drawn from white to black, the layer mask fades the layer out where the black becomes more predominant.
6 Update and close the image	

Topic D: Clipping masks and type masks

This topic covers the following Adobe ACA exam objectives for Photoshop CS5.

#	Objective
3.2a	Identify and label elements of the different types of layers.
3.2b	Demonstrate knowledge of masks and modes.
3.2c	Demonstrate knowledge of how to create masks.
4.7b	Demonstrate knowledge of functionality of type tools.
4.7c	Demonstrate knowledge of the uses of type layers.

Creating clipping masks

Explanation

When you create a *clipping mask*, you display the current layer over only the pixels in the layer below, as shown in Exhibit 2-4. The transparent space in the layer below—the base layer—specifies the areas that are masked in the layer above—the clipped layer.

Clipping masks work well when you want to mask a layer based on content that might change. For example, you can clip (attach) a layer to a type layer below it so that the clipping layer's contents are visible only over the text on the base layer. Because a clipping mask is dynamic, you can change the text in the layer below, and the effect is automatically updated.

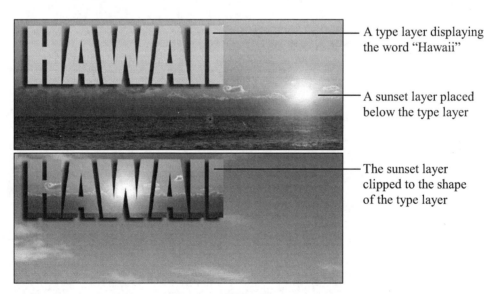

A type layer displaying the word "Hawaii"

A sunset layer placed below the type layer

The sunset layer clipped to the shape of the type layer

Exhibit 2-4: A clipping mask used with a type layer

A clipping mask can contain more than two layers. All of the layers clip to the shape of the base layer. To create a clipping mask:

1 Move the layer that you want to create a clipping mask for so that it's directly above the layer whose content you want it to clip to.

- Choose Layer, Create Clipping Mask.
- From the Layers panel menu, choose Create Clipping Mask.
- Press Alt, point between the two layers in the Layers panel, and click.

You can move the layers independently of one another. However, if you want them to move together, you can link them by selecting them both and clicking the Link layers button in the Layers panel.

To remove a clipping mask, you can use any of these techniques:

- Choose Layer, Release Clipping Mask.
- From the Layers panel menu, choose Release Clipping Mask.
- Press Alt, point to the line between the two layers in the Layers panel, and click.

Do it!

D-1:   Clipping a layer to an underlying layer

The files for this activity are in Student Data folder **Unit 2\Topic D**.

Here's how	Here's why
1 Open Hawaii 2	
Save the image as **My Hawaii 2**	In the current topic folder.
2 In the Layers panel, drag the Sunset layer above the HAWAII layer	You'll now clip the Sunset layer to the type layer below it, using the type layer as a clipping mask.
3 From the Layers panel menu, choose **Create Clipping Mask**	To create a clipping mask from the HAWAII layer. The Layers panel indicates which is the clipped layer.
4 Drag the Sunset layer to position the sun in the center of the "W" in "HAWAII"	
5 Press ⟨SHIFT⟩ and click the HAWAII layer	(In the Layers panel.) To select the Sunset and HAWAII layers so you can link them.
Click 🔗	(The Link layers button.) To link the two layers. Any time you move the content of either of these layers, the contents of both layers will move together.
6 In the image, drag the word **HAWAII**	To observe that the two layers move together.
7 Update the image	

The Type Mask tool

Explanation

Yet another way to create a mask is to use the Horizontal and Vertical Type Mask tools, located in the group with the Vertical Type tool. Essentially, these tools create a selection in the shape of the text you type, rather than a separate type layer. Once you're finished editing the text, you can apply adjustments either to the selection or to the image outside of the selection. You can save the selection as a channel so that you can use it later.

Do it!

D-2: Creating a type mask

The files for this activity are in Student Data folder **Unit 2\Topic D**.

Here's how	Here's why
1 Select the Cliffs layer	
2 In the Tools panel, click and hold ⊤	
Select the **Horizontal Type Mask** tool	
3 Click in the image	To create a mask.
4 Specify a font of **Times New Roman**, **Bold Italic**, **100 pt**	
Type **escape**	
5 Point away from the selection	The pointer indicates that you can move the text.
Drag the text to the center of the image	
6 On the options bar, click ✓	To commit the edits. The type becomes a selection.
7 In the Channels panel, click ⬚	To save the selection as a channel so that you can reuse it later, if desired.
8 Choose **Select**, **Inverse**	
In the Adjustments panel, click ▦	To create a Hue/Saturation adjustment layer.
Set the Saturation to **−50**	
Set the Lightness to **+50**	
9 Update and close the image	

Unit summary: Masks

Topic A   In this topic, you painted in **Quick Mask mode** to add to and subtract from a selection. You also painted in an **alpha channel** to modify a selection.

Topic B   In this topic, you created a **layer mask** to hide part of a layer. You also modified a layer mask.

Topic C   In this topic, you learned how to create a **grayscale mask** to partially mask a portion of an image.

Topic D   In this topic, you applied a **clipping mask** to mask one layer based on the contents of the layer below. You also learned how to use the **Horizontal Type Mask** tool to create a mask from text.

Independent practice activity

In this activity, you'll use Quick Mask mode to edit a selection. You'll also create a layer mask and a clipping mask. Finally, you'll apply a gradient layer mask.

The files for this activity are in Student Data folder **Unit 2\Unit summary**.

1 Open Chiles and save the image as **My chiles**.

2 Select the Magic Wand tool. Set the Tolerance to **32** and check **Contiguous**, if necessary. Click the white space surrounding the chiles. Press Shift and click the white space not selected in one or two places to get most of the surrounding area selected. Do not include the bowl in the selection.

3 Invert the selection so the chiles and the bowl are selected.

4 Edit the selection by painting in Quick Mask mode to improve the mask's accuracy. (*Hint:* Paint in black to add to the mask. Paint in white to add to the selection. Change brush size and hardness as needed.)

5 Double-click the Background layer and rename it as **Chile bowl** to convert it to a regular layer.

6 Display the image in Standard mode, and create a layer mask from the selection.

7 Open Turn up the heat, and save it as **My turn up the heat**.

8 Drag the Chiles image into the "My turn up the heat" image. (*Hint:* The layer mask will be copied along with the layer). Update and close the My chiles image.

9 In the Layers panel, drag the Chile bowl layer to the top of the layers, if necessary.

10 Use the Masks panel to adjust the Chile bowl layer mask by adding a 1 px feather.

11 Create a clipping mask with the Flames and HEAT layers so that the flames appear only within the outlines of the letters. Adjust the position of the flames within the letters. (*Hint:* First, move the Flames layer so that it's above the HEAT layer.)

12 Fade out the black part of the Outlander logo on the right with a gradient layer mask, as shown in Exhibit 2-5. (*Hint:* First, add a layer mask to the layer. Using the Gradient tool, specify settings and then drag to create the gradient.)

13 Update and close the image.

*Exhibit 2-5: The "My turn up the heat" image as it appears at the end of the
independent practice activity*

Review questions

1 How can you view a selection as a temporary colored overlay instead of as a marquee?

  A In the Tools panel, click the Edit in Quick Mask Mode button.

  B Choose View, Extras.

  C Choose View, Show, Selection Edges to uncheck it.

  D Choose View, Show, None.

2 In Quick Mask mode, how can you add to a selection?

  A Choose Select, Modify, Expand.

  B Choose Select, Grow.

  C Paint with white.

  D Paint with black.

3 How can you use the Channels panel to add to a saved selection?

  A While viewing the image, Ctrl+click the alpha channel containing the selection; then paint with white.

  B While viewing the image, Ctrl+click the alpha channel containing the selection; then paint with black.

  C Click the alpha channel containing the selection to display it in the image window; then paint with black.

  D Click the alpha channel containing the selection to display it in the image window; then paint with white.

4 To view an alpha channel's contents as a colored overlay over the original image, you should:

  A Alt+click it.

  B Select it and enter Quick Mask mode.

  C Select it and view the composite RGB channels at the same time.

  D Choose View, Extras.

5 Which key do you press while clicking a layer mask thumbnail in the Layers panel to view the mask in the image window?

  A Alt

  B Ctrl

  C Shift

  D Caps Lock

6 Gray pixels in a layer mask make the corresponding image pixels:

  A More gray

  B Semi-transparent

  C Hard-edged

  D Inverted

7 Name three ways to create gray pixels within a layer mask.

8 Which layer in a clipping group defines the shape to which the others are clipped?

  A The top layer in the clipping group

  B The bottom layer in the clipping group

  C The one you select when you apply the clipping mask

  D The one you hide by clicking in the visibility column

9 Which methods can you use to create a clipping mask? [Choose all that apply.]

  A Press Alt, point to the line between two layers in the Layers panel, and click.

  B Create the bottom layer and choose Layer, Clip Layer Above to This One.

  C Select the layer that you want to clip to the layer below and choose Layer, Create Clipping Mask.

  D Select two layers and choose Layer, Group Layers.

Unit 3

Vector paths

Unit time: 70 minutes

Complete this unit, and you'll know how to:

A Use the path tools and commands to create vector paths.

B Use the path tools and options to edit vector paths.

C Use paths to create vector masks and clipping paths.

D Use paths to create vector-based artwork.

Topic A: Creating vector paths

This topic covers the following Adobe ACA exam objectives for Photoshop CS5.

#	Objective
3.1c	Demonstrate knowledge of the functions of tools on the Tools panel.
4.1d	Demonstrate knowledge of selection commands and how to modify selections.
4.6a	Demonstrate knowledge of drawing by creating shape layers and paths.

Uses for vector paths

Explanation

Most images you work with in Photoshop are probably made up entirely of pixels. However, you can also create *vector path*s to define lines and areas geometrically. Purposes for which you would use vector paths might include:

- Selecting and masking image areas that have clearly defined shapes, such as straight lines or smooth curves.
- Creating geometric graphics that are easy to draw and modify.
- Adding *clipping paths* to define transparent areas in an image that you plan to place in another application for print use.
- Flowing text or brush shapes along a path.

Using vector paths as selection masks and layer masks

When you want to select or mask part of an image that has a geometric shape or is very detailed, you'll often get more accurate results by using vector paths. You can't directly use a vector path to partially mask image pixels, as you can by painting with gray in an alpha channel, in a pixel-based layer mask, or in Quick Mask mode. However, after creating a path in the shape of the area you want to select or mask, you can convert the vector path to a selection or layer mask.

Drawing geometric graphics

You can also use vector paths to draw geometric graphics in an image. Using the shape and Pen tools, you can create geometric graphics that are easier to modify and reshape than are pixel-based areas created with the Brush or Pencil tools. When you flatten an image containing shape layers, the image's appearance doesn't change, but the vector paths themselves are removed, leaving only pixels.

Flowing type or brush shapes along a path

You can also use vector paths as guides for flowing text. For example, you can create text along a curving path. In addition, you can apply a stroke to the path based on a brush shape. The path then looks like it was drawn with the Brush tool.

Creating clipping paths

You might use Photoshop to create an image for use in another program. However, not all programs will support transparency in the image. To ensure that an image retains transparency when exported to a print application, use a vector path as a clipping path that specifies the visible area, leaving the area outside the clipping path transparent.

Do it!

A-1:   Discussing the uses of vector paths

Questions and answers

1 In what circumstances might you want to use vector paths to specify an image selection?

2 What is a benefit of drawing with the Pen and shape tools instead of painting with the Brush or Pencil tools?

3 What is the purpose of using a vector path as a clipping path?

The Freeform Pen tool

Explanation

The *Pen tools* and *path editing tools* are stored in the group that shows the Pen tool by default, as shown in Exhibit 3-1. They include the Freeform Pen tool, which you can use to draw paths of any shape, much as you can use the Lasso tool to create selections of any shape. When you select the Freeform Pen tool, the options bar displays the options shown in Exhibit 3-2.

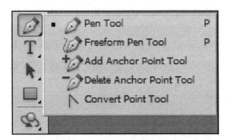

Exhibit 3-1: The pen and path editing tools

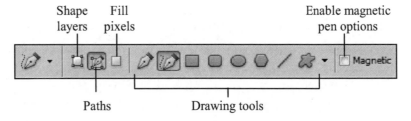

Exhibit 3-2: Some of the Freeform Pen tool options on the options bar

Several of the Freeform Pen tool options are described in the following table.

Item	Description
Shape layers icon	When this icon is selected, the paths you create generate *shape layers*. You can use a shape layer to add shapes filled with the current foreground color or filled with a style that applies a gradient or pattern.
Paths icon	When this icon is selected, the paths you create generate *work paths*. You can use work paths to create vector paths that make no visible change in the image but can be used to create selections or clipping paths.
Fill pixels icon	When this icon is selected, the shapes you draw are painted directly on the current layer as pixels, rather than as vector paths. You can't modify these shapes by using the vector editing tools, but you can modify them as you'd modify any other raster data. This option is available with the shape tools, but not with the Pen tools.
Drawing tool icons	Click a drawing tool icon to select that tool.
Enable magnetic pen options	When enabled, this setting converts the Freeform Pen tool to the Magnetic Pen tool so that the path you create automatically snaps to the image based on settings you specify. The Magnetic Pen tool operates similarly to the Magnetic Lasso tool.

To use the Magnetic Pen tool to draw a freeform vector path:

1　Select the Freeform Pen tool.

2　On the options bar, check Magnetic.

3　Point to where you want to begin the path, and click to add the first *fastening point*, which indicates where the path begins.

4　Move the pointer within the image to specify the shape of the path. As you move the pointer, fastening points appear along the path to specify where it flows. You can click to add a fastening point where you want one, and you can press Backspace or Delete to remove the last fastening point added.

5　Point to the first fastening point (where you started the path), and when the pointer displays a small circle, click to close the path. You can also double-click at any time to complete the path with a segment connecting the last fastening point to the first one.

Saving paths

When you create a path with the Paths option selected on the options bar, the new path is added as a work path, as shown in Exhibit 3-3. The work path is visible in the image, and it appears in the Paths panel with the name "Work Path."

The work path you've created is temporary. If you click a blank part of the Paths panel to deselect the work path and then draw a new path, the new one will replace the old one. However, you can save a work path as a permanent path:

1　In the Paths panel, double-click Work Path to open the Save Path dialog box.

2　In the Name box, enter a name for the path.

3　Click OK.

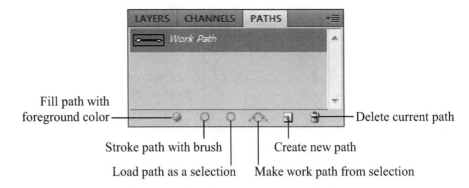

Fill path with foreground color ——

Delete current path

Stroke path with brush

Create new path

Load path as a selection

Make work path from selection

Exhibit 3-3: The Paths panel

Path components

Paths created in Photoshop are made up of anchor points, segments, and direction points, as shown in Exhibit 3-4. The *anchor points* determine where the path flows. A *segment* is the part of a path between two anchor points. *Direction points* determine the curvature (if any) of each segment.

Direction points extend from anchor points. Each anchor point can have two direction points, with each one controlling the curvature of the segment on either side of the anchor point. If a segment contains no curvature, its anchor points won't have associated direction points.

Anchor point ——

Direction point ——

Segment

Exhibit 3-4: The components of a vector path

Selecting paths and path components

The *selection tools* are stored in the group that shows the Path Selection tool by default, as shown in Exhibit 3-5. The technique you use to select a path depends on what you want to do with it:

- To show a path in the image window, click the path in the Paths panel. You can then create a selection from the path, apply or adjust a fill or stroke, and more. To hide any paths in the image, click a blank area of the Paths panel.

- To display a path's anchor points, click the path with the Path Selection tool. You can then drag the path to move it.

- To display a path's associated direction points, click a segment or anchor point with the Direct Selection tool. You can then drag direction points and anchor points to reshape the path.

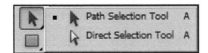

Exhibit 3-5: The selection tools

Do it!

A-2: Creating a freeform path

The files for this activity are in Student Data folder **Unit 3\Topic A**.

Here's how	Here's why
1 Open Spoon 1	
Save the image as **My spoon 1**	(In the current topic folder.) You'll use the Freeform Pen tool to draw a path that traces the outline of the spoon.
Choose **View**, **Fit on Screen**	
2 In the Tools panel, click and hold	To display the Pen tools.
Select the **Freeform Pen Tool**	
On the options bar, verify that the Paths icon is selected	To specify that the paths you draw will generate work paths, rather than shape layers.
On the options bar, check **Magnetic**	To convert the Freeform Pen tool to the Magnetic Pen tool. A small horseshoe magnet is added to the pointer icon.
3 Click an edge of the spoon	To place the first fastening point, which determines where the path begins.

4 Move the pointer around the spoon	Additional fastening points appear along the path as you move the pointer.
When the pointer is over the initial fastening point, click the mouse	
	(Point to the initial fastening point, and when the pointer displays a small circle, click.) To close the path.
5 Click the **Paths** panel	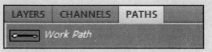
	The path you just created appears as Work Path. You'll save the work path.
6 In the Paths panel, double-click **Work Path**	To open the Save Path dialog box.
Edit the Name box to read **Spoon freeform**	
Click **OK**	To save the path.
7 Zoom in on the image	To observe the inaccuracies in the path.
8 In the Tools panel, click	(The Path Selection tool.) You can use the Path Selection tool to select and manipulate a path.
Click the edge of the path as shown	
	To select the path so that its anchor points are visible.
Click in the image window, away from the path	To deselect the path anchor points.
9 Click a blank area in the Paths panel	To deselect the path. It's no longer visible in the image window.
10 Update the image	

Converting selections to paths

Explanation

Another way to create a path is to convert a selection to a path. This method is particularly useful when you want to generate a path for an item that you can easily select with the selection tools.

To convert a selection to a path, click the "Make work path from selection" icon in the Paths panel. The new path is created with the default settings. If you want to control how accurately the path matches the shape of the original selection, then before you convert the selection to a path, change settings in the Make Work Path dialog box.

To open the Make Work Path dialog box, do either of the following:

- From the Paths panel menu, choose Make Work Path.
- Press Alt and click the "Make work path from selection" icon.

In the Make Work Path dialog box, you can specify a Tolerance value. The lower the tolerance, the more closely the path will match the shape of the original selection. In addition, a lower tolerance will generate a path with more anchor points. A higher tolerance will generate a smoother path with fewer anchor points, but the path won't conform as closely to the original shape of the selection.

Do it!

A-3: Converting a selection to a path

Here's how	Here's why
1 In the Layers panel, select the Spoon layer	If necessary.
2 Select the Magic Wand tool	
Set the Tolerance value to **60**	
Press CTRL + 0	To zoom out and make the image fit the screen.
3 Click the spoon, as shown	
Press SHIFT and click other areas on the measuring spoon to add to the selection	To select all areas of the spoon.
4 Select the Lasso tool	
Press SHIFT and drag around the spices in the spoon	
	(Drag around any other areas necessary.) To add them to the selection.

5 In the Paths panel, click ⬡	(The "Make work path from selection" icon.) To create a path from the selection you just made.
Double-click **Work Path**	To open the Save Path dialog box.
Name the path **Spoon selection**	Double-click the path name, edit the Name box, and click OK.
6 In the Tools panel, click ▶	The Path Selection tool.
In the image window, click the path	To observe the number of points and the accuracy and smoothness of the path.
	You'll deselect the path and create a second, more accurate path.
Deselect the path	In the Paths panel, click a blank area below the path.
7 Choose **Select**, **Reselect**	To select the most recent selection.
From the Paths panel menu, choose **Make Work Path...**	To open the Make Work Path dialog box.
Edit the Tolerance box to read **1**	
Click **OK**	To create the work path.
Name the work path **Spoon selection 1 pixel**	
8 Using the Path Selection tool, select the path you just created	Observe that the path is more accurate, but contains more points.
Deselect the path	Click a blank area of the Paths panel.
9 Update the image	

The Pen tool

Explanation

Another way to create a path is to use the Pen tool. When you use the Pen tool to create a path, you have more control over the path's shape than you do with other methods. With the Pen tool, you specify the location of anchor points and direction points to create straight or curving segments with precision.

Straight segments

To create a straight segment, click to place two anchor points, as shown in Exhibit 3-6. A straight segment appears between the two anchor points, and there are no direction points. You can continue clicking to add more segments to the path.

To begin a new path, press Esc or click the Pen tool in the Tools panel. A small "×" appears next to the Pen tool's pointer when it's ready to begin a new path. To draw a horizontal, vertical, or 45-degree segment, press Shift as you click to add the second anchor point.

Exhibit 3-6: A straight segment connecting two anchor points

Curving segments

To create a curving segment, point to where you want to begin the path. Click and drag in the direction you want the path to curve. Point to where you want to add the second anchor point, and drag in the direction you want the path to move as it enters the second anchor point.

For example, to create a rainbow shape, drag up to indicate that the path should curve upward from the first anchor point, as shown in Exhibit 3-7. Point to where you want to place the second anchor point, and drag down to indicate that the path should curve downward as it enters that anchor point, as shown in Exhibit 3-8.

Exhibit 3-7: The first anchor point and direction point for a curving segment

Exhibit 3-8: A curving segment

Smooth points and corner points

When you drag to create an anchor point with a direction point, a second direction point is created to control the curvature of the next segment. By default, the next segment will continue the first segment's curve direction. So if a segment curves downward into its second anchor point, the path will continue to curve downward as it leaves that anchor point for the next segment. When the segments on either side of an anchor point curve in the same direction, that anchor point is called a *smooth point*, shown in Exhibit 3-9.

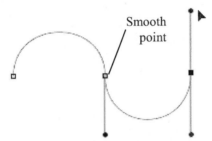

Exhibit 3-9: Two segments connected by a smooth point

You can specify a different direction for the second segment, thereby creating a *corner point*. To draw a path's second segment with a corner point, press Alt to temporarily select the Convert Point tool, and drag the existing direction point for the next segment to specify the direction you want the next segment to curve in, as shown in Exhibit 3-10.

You can then release Alt to return to the Pen tool, and drag to specify the ending anchor point and direction point for the segment, as shown in Exhibit 3-11. Dragging a direction point with the Convert Point tool converts a smooth point to a corner point. You can do this while drawing a path or after a path is complete.

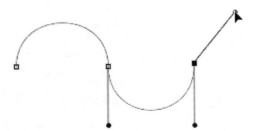

Exhibit 3-10: Dragging a direction point with the Convert Point tool to specify a corner point

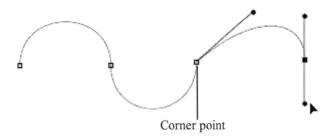

Corner point

Exhibit 3-11: Two segments connected by a corner point

If you click twice to create a straight segment, you can drag from the second anchor point to create a single direction point to specify the curvature for the next segment, without affecting the existing straight segment.

In addition, if you want to draw a straight segment following a curving segment, you can press Alt and click the curving segment's second anchor point to remove the direction point that would have applied curvature to the following segment. The existing curving segment won't be affected.

Do it!

A-4: Creating paths with the Pen tool

Here's how	Here's why
1 Choose **View**, **Fit on Screen**	If necessary.
In the Tools panel, click and hold	The Freeform Pen tool.
Select the **Pen Tool**	You'll begin drawing a path around the spoon by creating a straight segment along the spoon's top edge.
2 Click as shown	To place the first anchor point of the straight segment. After you click to add the first point, the pointer's "×" symbol disappears to indicate that additional clicks will add to this path, rather than begin a new path.
3 Click as shown	To complete the initial straight segment.

4   From the anchor point you just
    created, drag left and slightly up,
    as shown

To create the initial point of a curved segment.

5   Click and hold as shown

Hold the mouse button down.

Drag down and slightly to the left,
as shown, and then release the
mouse

To create the curved segment around the top of
the spoon's well.

6   Click and hold as shown

Hold the mouse button down.

Drag up and to right, as shown,
and then release the mouse

To create the curved segment at the bottom of
the spoon.

7   Press (ALT) and drag the top-right
    direction point you just created, as
    shown

To allow the right direction point to move at an
independent angle, letting you create a sharp
corner.

8   Click as shown

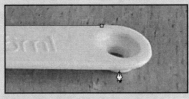

To create a straight segment at the bottom of the spoon.

9   From the anchor point you just created, drag right as shown

To begin a curved segment for the end of the spoon.

10 On the first anchor point you created, drag left as shown

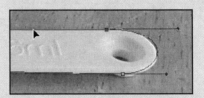

To complete the path.

11 In the Paths panel, save the work path as **Spoon pen**

12 Update and close the image

Topic B: Editing vector paths

This topic covers the following Adobe ACA exam objectives for Photoshop CS5.

#	Objective
3.1c	Demonstrate knowledge of the functions of tools on the Tools panel.
4.6a	Demonstrate knowledge of drawing by creating shape layers and paths.
4.6b	Demonstrate knowledge of how to edit a path.

Modifying paths

Explanation

After creating a path, you can change its shape. You can add and remove anchor points and direction points, convert smooth points to corner points, and drag segments, anchor points, and direction points.

The Direct Selection tool

To modify a path, you can use the Direct Selection tool and the following techniques:

- Drag a curving segment to increase or decrease its curvature without changing the angle of the direction points.
- Drag a direction point to adjust the curvature of its associated segment.
- Drag an anchor point to move it; this adjusts the segments on either side of the anchor point.

When you drag a direction point attached to a smooth point, the other direction point connected to the anchor point moves as well. To move a direction point independently, use the Convert Point tool to drag it. When you use the Convert Point tool to drag a direction point, you convert the smooth point to a corner point.

Do it!

B-1: Adjusting path points

The files for this activity are in Student Data folder **Unit 3\Topic B**.

Here's how	Here's why
1 Open Spoon 2	
Save the image as **My spoon 2**	In the current topic folder.
2 Zoom in to 300% on the bowl of the spoon	
3 In the Tools panel, click and hold	The Path Selection tool.
Select the **Direct Selection Tool**	You'll drag segments, anchor points, and direction points to adjust the path's shape.

4 In the Paths panel, select **Spoon pen**	To activate the path in the image.
Click the path	To select it and view the anchor points.
5 Drag the anchor points to just inside the edges of the spoon	If necessary.
6 At the top of the spoon, adjust the positions of the anchor and direction points, as shown	

To make the path match the spoon fairly closely. Press Alt to drag individual direction points.

At the left side of the spoon, adjust the positions of the anchor and direction points, as shown	
At the bottom of the spoon, adjust the positions of the anchor and direction points, as shown	

7 Update the image

Adding and removing anchor points

Explanation

After completing a path, you can add or remove anchor points. To add a point, you can select the Pen tool or the Add Anchor Point tool, point to any path segment, and click. When you use the Pen tool to point to a path segment, the pointer displays a plus sign (+), indicating that clicking will add an anchor point.

You can remove an anchor point by using either the Pen tool or the Delete Anchor Point tool; just point to the anchor point and click. When you use the Pen tool to point to an anchor point, the mouse pointer displays a minus sign (−), indicating that clicking will delete the anchor point.

Do it!

B-2: Changing the number of anchor points

Here's how	Here's why
1 Scroll to the right end of the spoon	
2 Try to drag the rightmost path segment to match the spoon	Observe that the path can't match the shape precisely with only the two points defining the curved segment.
3 Using the Pen tool, click as shown	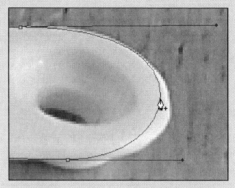 To add another anchor point to the curve.
4 Using the Direct Selection tool, drag to position the anchor point and its direction points in the positions and angles shown	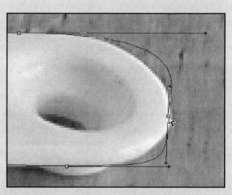 The anchor point controls the position of the path. The direction points control the severity and angle of the curve.
5 Drag the anchor points and direction points as necessary to closely match the spoon curvature	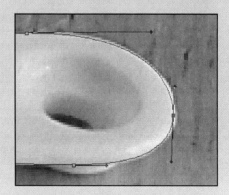
Update the image	

Subpaths

Explanation

When a path is selected in the Paths panel, any new paths you create are added as *subpaths*. Creating subpaths is useful when you want to use paths to generate a selection or create a mask made up of more than one area or shape. When you create subpaths, you can use buttons on the options bar, shown in Exhibit 3-12, to specify how the paths will interact with each other where they overlap.

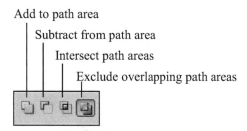

Exhibit 3-12: Buttons on the options bar for combining subpaths

The buttons for combining subpaths are described in the following table.

Button	Description
Add to path area	The area within new subpaths you draw is added to the original path. A selection or mask generated from the paths includes the area within all of the paths.
Subtract from path area	New subpaths you draw remove any part of the original path that they overlap. A selection or mask generated from the paths includes only the area of the original path that's not overlapped by any of the subpaths.
Intersect path areas	A new subpath you draw restricts the path to the area where it intersects with the original path. A selection or mask generated from the paths includes only the area where they intersect.
Exclude overlapping path areas	A new subpath you draw is added to the path area, but overlapping areas are removed. A selection or mask generated from the paths includes the area within all paths, except for the areas where they overlap.

After creating a path, you can apply a different path area button to it. To do so, use the Path Selection tool to select the subpath, and click the path area button you want.

Converting paths to selections

You can convert a path in the Paths panel to a selection by using either of these techniques:

- Select the path in the Paths panel and then click the "Load path as a selection" button.
- Press Ctrl and click the path in the Paths panel.

Do it!

B-3:   Combining subpaths to form a single path

Here's how	Here's why
1 Select the Pen tool	You'll create a small hole in the spoon because you want the background to show through it when you use the path as a mask.
2 In the Paths panel, verify that the Spoon pen path is selected	You'll add a subpath to it.
3 Create an anchor point and direction points, as shown	
Create a second anchor point and direction points, as shown	
Press (ALT) and drag the second direction point of the anchor point you just created, as shown	 To make a sharp corner in the path.
Press (ALT) and click the initial point of the path	 To create another sharp corner.
4 On the options bar, verify that the "Exclude overlapping path areas" button is selected	 This option will cause the new subpath to cut a hole in the original path when you load it as a selection.
5 Press (CTRL) and click **Spoon pen** in the Paths panel	To load the path as a selection.
Choose **Select, Inverse**	To invert the selection.
Press (← BACKSPACE)	To delete the background. The black layer created below the spoon shows through the hole.
Press (CTRL) + (Z)	To bring back the background.
Deselect the current selection	You'll now add another subpath to create the bump at the bottom of the spoon handle.

6 In the Paths panel, select **Spoon pen** | When a path is selected, any new path you create acts as a subpath.

7 In the Tools panel, click and hold [▢] | The Rectangle tool.

Select the **Ellipse Tool**

On the options bar, verify that the Paths option is selected

Drag to create a path, as shown

8 Select the Path Selection tool

9 Press [CTRL] and click **Spoon pen** | (In the Paths panel.) To convert the paths to a selection.

Invert the selection | Choose Select, Inverse.

Press [← BACKSPACE] | To delete the background. The black layer below shows through the top half of the ellipse, which wasn't your intent.

Press [CTRL] + [Z] | To restore the background.

Deselect the current selection | You'll apply the "Add to path area" option to this subpath.

10 Click **Spoon pen** | (In the Paths panel.) To select the path.

Using the Path Selection tool, click the ellipse path | This path should add to, and not exclude, the original path.

On the options bar, click [⬚] | The "Add to shape area" button.

11 Press [CTRL] and click **Spoon pen** | (In the Paths panel.) To convert the path to a selection.

Invert the selection

Press [← BACKSPACE] | To delete the background. The elliptical subpath now adds to the shape area, as you intended.

Press [CTRL] + [Z] | To restore the background

12 Update and close the image

Topic C: Vector masks

This topic covers the following Adobe ACA exam objectives for Photoshop CS5.

#	Objective
3.2b	Demonstrate knowledge of masks and modes.
3.2c	Demonstrate knowledge of how to create masks.

Creating vector masks

Explanation

In addition to using vector paths to create selections, you can use vector paths to create vector masks. You can also use vector paths to generate layer masks and clipping paths.

A *vector mask* is similar to a layer mask, but with the following differences:

Factor	Layer mask	Vector mask
Visibility control	Use selection tools or paint on the mask to control visibility. White makes areas visible; black, invisible; and gray, partially transparent.	Use Pen or shape tools to control what is hidden and what is visible.
Edges	Gradients and soft transitions are available between areas.	Crisp, sharp lines occur between areas.
Scaling	Rasterized (bitmap) areas are resolution-dependent; scaling up or down can produce choppy edges.	Vector-based areas are resolution-independent and scale up and down smoothly.
Ease and accuracy of modification	Brushes and selection tools provide reasonable accuracy and are relatively easy to use.	Pen and shape tools are easier to use and more precise than brushes or selection tools.

After creating a path, you can load it as a selection and create a standard layer mask from the selection. A single layer can include both a vector mask and a layer mask.

To create a vector mask from a path:

1 In the Paths panel, select the path that you want to use as a mask.

2 In the Layers panel, select the layer you want to mask.

3 Choose Layer, Vector Mask, Current Path.

Clipping paths

You might use images from Photoshop in documents designed for print use. If an image in Photoshop includes transparent areas, those areas remain transparent when you print the image from many other programs, including Adobe InDesign and Adobe Illustrator.

However, some programs, such as QuarkXPress, don't support Photoshop's transparency and will print transparent areas from the image as solid colored areas. In those cases, you can use Photoshop to specify a *clipping path*, which specifies that only areas within it are printed, leaving areas outside the clipping path transparent.

When you add a clipping path to an image in Photoshop, you have to save the image in Photoshop, EPS, or TIFF format. You cannot use clipping paths to specify transparent areas for Web graphics. When you want to create Web images with transparent areas, you can use the GIF and PNG formats, which support transparency.

Flatness

When you create a clipping path, you can specify a *flatness* value for it. Generally, you can leave this value blank. However, you might experience errors when printing to a PostScript printer. If that happens, and you're printing to a low-resolution printer, use a flatness value of about 3; for high-resolution printers, use a flatness value of up to 10. The flatness value specifies how many straight segments are used to reproduce the curve of a clipping path. The smaller the segments, the more of them are needed to reproduce the curve, resulting in a smoother curve but requiring more memory during printing. A higher flatness value produces curves that use fewer straight segments, thereby requiring less memory during printing.

Specifying a clipping path

To create a clipping path:

1 From the Paths panel menu, choose Clipping Path to open the Clipping Path dialog box.
2 From the Path list, select the path you want to convert to a clipping path.
3 In the Flatness box, enter a flatness value.
4 Click OK.

Do it!

C-1: Creating a vector mask

The files for this activity are in Student Data folder **Unit 3\Topic C**.

Here's how	Here's why
1 Open Spoon 3	
Save the image as **My spoon 3**	In the current topic folder.
2 In the Layers panel, select the Spoon layer	If necessary.
3 In the Paths panel, select the Spoon pen path	
4 Choose **Layer**, **Vector Mask**, **Current Path**	The black background from the layer below appears around the spoon.
	You can modify the vector mask at any time by using the path tools.
5 In the Layers panel, press (SHIFT) and click the vector mask thumbnail	To disable the vector mask.
6 Update and close the image	

Topic D: Paths for creative imagery

This topic covers the following Adobe ACA exam objectives for Photoshop CS5.

#	Objective
4.6a	Demonstrate knowledge of drawing by creating shape layers and paths.
4.6b	Demonstrate knowledge of how to edit a path.
4.6d	Identify tools that are used for drawing, or creating shapes.
4.7c	Demonstrate knowledge of the uses of type layers.

Paths as graphics

Explanation

In addition to creating paths as clipping paths, as masks, or for generating selections, you can create paths as actual graphics that appear in your image. For example, you can adjust the shape of text characters, create a path on which to flow text, apply a brush stroke to a path, or create vector shapes that display a fill.

Converting type to paths

The font files you use to create text define each character as a vector path. Ordinarily, you don't see or adjust the points and path segments, but they're used to generate the shapes with smooth edges at any size. Photoshop allows you to convert type layers back to the original vector paths, which you can then adjust to change the character shapes, as shown in Exhibit 3-13.

To convert type to a path:

1   Select the type layer.

2   Either right-click the type layer or choose Layer, Type. Then choose a command to convert the type:

- If you want to replace the type layer with a shape layer that looks identical (but has editable path shapes), choose Convert to Shape.

- If you want the type layer to remain, and you want to add the path outlines to the Paths panel as the work path, choose Create Work Path.

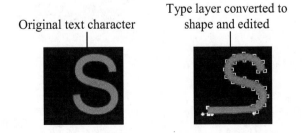

Original text character   Type layer converted to shape and edited

Exhibit 3-13: Type converted to a shape

Do it!

D-1: Converting type characters to editable shapes

The files for this activity are in Student Data folder **Unit 3\Topic D**.

Here's how	Here's why
1 Open Outlander ad	
Save the image as **My Outlander ad**	(In the current topic folder.) You'll extend the bottom-left side of the "S" in "Spices" to the left edge of the image. First, you'll duplicate the Spices layer to retain the original version.
2 Drag the **Spices** layer to the "Create a new layer" icon	To create a "Spices copy" layer.
Hide the Spices layer	You can revert to this layer later, if necessary.
3 Right-click the **Spices copy** layer and choose **Convert to Shape**	To convert the type to a shape layer with a vector mask in the shape of the text characters.
4 Using the Direct Selection tool, click the **S** at the beginning of "Spices"	 You'll delete some anchor points at the bottom-left side in order to extend the bottom of the character to the left.
5 Drag a marquee to select the last six anchor points, as shown	
Press (DELETE)	
6 Drag a selection marquee around the two bottom-left anchor points, as shown	
7 Press (SHIFT) and drag the bottommost anchor point to the left edge of the image, as shown	
8 Update the image	

Type on a path

Explanation

To add text that flows along a path:

1 In the Tools panel, select a Type tool.

2 In the Paths panel, select the path you want the text to flow along.

3 In the image window, click the path at the location where you want to begin adding text. A flashing insertion point appears. A new type layer appears in the Layers panel. A new type path appears in the Paths panel, containing a copy of the original path you clicked.

4 Specify the text formatting you want on the options bar, and type to add the text that will flow along the path.

You can also click within a closed path to add type that flows within the path.

Do it!

D-2: Wrapping type on a path

The files for this activity are in Student Data folder **Unit 3\Topic D**.

Here's how	Here's why
1 Open Spoon 4	This image contains a layer with a mask, but the mask is disabled. You'll place the Spoon layer in the My Outlander ad image.
Arrange the image windows so that you can see both images	
Drag the Spoon layer into the My Outlander ad image	
Close Spoon 4	
2 Position the Spoon layer as shown	
3 In the Layers panel, press (SHIFT) and click the vector mask thumbnail	To activate the vector mask, hiding the image outside the spoon.
4 In the Paths panel, select the Spoon Vector Mask path	
5 Press (D)	To select the default colors.
Press (X)	To exchange the foreground and background colors.

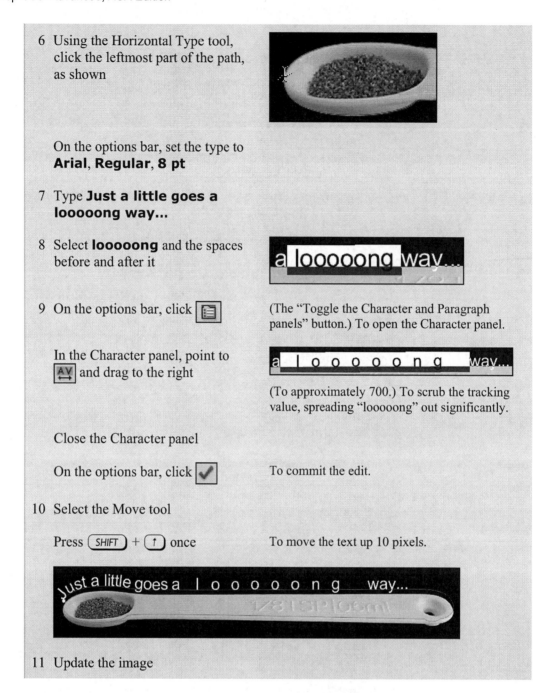

6 Using the Horizontal Type tool, click the leftmost part of the path, as shown

On the options bar, set the type to **Arial**, **Regular**, **8 pt**

7 Type **Just a little goes a looooong way...**

8 Select **looooong** and the spaces before and after it

9 On the options bar, click ▤ (The "Toggle the Character and Paragraph panels" button.) To open the Character panel.

In the Character panel, point to ꜜ and drag to the right

(To approximately 700.) To scrub the tracking value, spreading "looooong" out significantly.

Close the Character panel

On the options bar, click ✔ To commit the edit.

10 Select the Move tool

Press (SHIFT) + (↑) once To move the text up 10 pixels.

11 Update the image

Shape layers

Explanation You can also use vector paths to draw geometric graphics in an image. You can use Photoshop's shape tools or Pen tools to draw a shape, so that a new shape layer is created automatically. The shape tools are stored in the group that shows the Rectangle tool by default, as shown in Exhibit 3-14.

A *shape layer* is actually a solid fill layer with a vector mask. Creating shapes by using a shape layer is useful when you want to be able to easily edit and scale the shape with path editing tools.

To draw filled shapes by using the shape tools:

1 In the Tools panel or on the options bar (if a shape or Pen tool is already selected), select a shape tool.

2 On the options bar, click the Shape Layers button.

3 On the options bar, use the Style list to specify a fill style for the shape, if you want to use one.

4 In the image, drag to create the shape.

5 Double-click the new shape layer to open the Layer Style dialog box. Apply custom styles to the shape, and click OK.

■	Rectangle Tool	U
	Rounded Rectangle Tool	U
	Ellipse Tool	U
	Polygon Tool	U
	Line Tool	U
	Custom Shape Tool	U

Exhibit 3-14: The shape tools

Do it!

D-3: Creating a vector shape layer

Here's how	Here's why
1 In the Layers panel, create a new layer below the Spoon layer	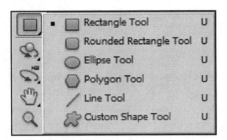
2 Select the Ellipse tool	
On the options bar, click [icon]	The Custom Shape tool.
In the Custom Shape picker, select the indicated shape	
	The Starburst shape.
On the options bar, click [icon]	The Shape layers button.

3 Create a starburst shape, as shown

4 Double-click the **Shape 1** layer	To open the Layer Style dialog box.
Under Styles, click **Gradient Overlay**	To display the Gradient Overlay settings.
From the Gradient list, select **Orange, Yellow, Orange**	
5 Click **OK**	To close the Layer Style dialog box.
6 In the Paths panel, click below the last path	To deselect the vector mask.
7 Update the image	

Creating a brush stroke from a path

Explanation

Another way to use a path as an artistic element in an image is to create a brush stroke based on the path's shape. When you create a brush stroke based on a path, the stroke follows the shape of all paths and subpaths, regardless of the options you specified for how the subpaths interact.

If a path includes overlapping subpaths, and you want to apply a brush stroke to only the outer border of the overlapping paths, you should first combine the overlapping subpaths into a single path.

Applying a brush stroke to paths

To apply a brush stroke to a path:

1 In the Paths panel, select the path you want to stroke. If the path includes overlapping subpaths that you want to combine, then follow these steps:

    a If you want to keep a copy of the original path with the subpaths, drag the path to the Create new path button in the Paths panel to make a copy.

    b In the duplicate path, use the Path Selection tool to select each subpath you want to combine.

    c On the options bar, click Combine.

2 In the Layers panel, select the layer that you want the stroke to appear on.

3 In the Tools panel, select the Brush tool.

4 In the Brush Preset picker, select the brush you want to use.

5 In the Paths panel, click the "Stroke path with brush" button.

Do it!   **D-4: Stroking a path with a brush shape**

Here's how	Here's why
1 Select the Spoon layer	
2 In the Paths panel, drag **Spoon Vector Mask** to the Create new path button	To duplicate the path. You'll experiment with making a creative stroked outline of the measuring spoon.
Name the duplicate path **Spoon combined**	
3 Hide the Spoon layer	
4 Above the Spoon layer, create a layer named **Drawn spoon**	
5 Set the foreground color to white	(If necessary.) Press X.
6 Select the Path Selection tool	
Press SHIFT and click the spoon outline and the ellipse	
On the options bar, click **Combine**	To combine the two paths into a single path. The overlapping areas are removed.
7 Select the Brush tool	
Select the 33-pixel **Hard Pastel on Canvas** brush, as shown	 From the Brush Preset picker.
In the Paths panel, click ⬭	The "Stroke path with brush" button.
In the Paths panel, click below the last path	To deselect all paths.
8 Update and close the image	

Unit summary: Vector paths

Topic A   In this topic, you learned about the uses of **vector paths** in Photoshop. You also learned how to use the Pen tools to draw paths, and you **converted selections to paths**. Finally, you saved paths by using the Paths panel.

Topic B   In this topic, you used the Direct Selection tool to **edit paths** by adjusting anchor points, direction points, and segments. You also added and removed anchor points, and you created **subpaths**.

Topic C   In this topic, you used **vector masks** to mask layer content. You also designated a path as a **clipping path** to specify transparent areas of an image that will be printed from a desktop publishing application.

Topic D   In this topic, you **converted type to paths** and wrapped type along a path. In addition, you used the shape tools to add **shape layers** to an image, and you applied layer styles to the shapes. Finally, you created brush strokes that flowed along the shape of a path.

Independent practice activity

In this activity, you'll create a path and a subpath. In addition, you'll use a path to create a clipping path and a vector mask.

The files for this activity are in Student Data folder **Unit 3\Unit summary**.

1 Open Spice bottle and save the image as **My spice bottle**.

2 Using the Pen tool, create a path from the top-left corner of the bottle, down around the bottle bottom, and up to the top-right corner, as shown in Exhibit 3-15. Don't include the top curve.

3 Using the Ellipse tool, make a subpath for the top of the bottle, as shown in Exhibit 3-16. (*Hint:* Specify the "Add to path area" option for the ellipse.)

4 Save the work path as a path named **Bottle**.

5 Specify that the path act as a clipping path to specify transparency outside the bottle when you place the image in a file for print use. (*Hint:* Use a flatness value of 10 for high-resolution printing.)

6 Make this path a vector mask for the Bottle layer, as shown in Exhibit 3-17. (*Hint:* Be sure the Bottle layer is selected in the Layers panel, and the Bottle path is selected in the Paths panel. Then choose the command.)

7 Update and close all images.

Exhibit 3-15: The path as it appears after Step 2

Exhibit 3-16: The path as it appears after Step 3

Exhibit 3-17: The path as it appears after Step 6

Review questions

1 Which tool cannot directly create a vector path?

A Pen

B Rectangle

C Custom Shape

D Lasso

2 How can you create a shape layer that displays an oval filled with a solid color?

A Select the Elliptical Marquee tool and drag in the image.

B Select the Ellipse tool and drag in the image.

C Select the Lasso tool and drag in the image.

D Create a new layer; then select the Elliptical Marquee tool and drag in the image.

3 True or false? A vector path must pass through each direction point.

4 To choose exactly where anchor and direction points will be placed along a vector path as you create it, which tool should you use?

A The Ellipse tool

B The Lasso tool

C The Polygon tool

D The Pen tool

5 Which of the following are advantages of using vector drawing tools versus using raster drawing tools? [Choose all that apply.]

    A You can add or remove selected areas in Quick Mask mode.

    B You can select and mask image areas that have clearly defined shapes, such as smoothly flowing curves.

    C You can create paths in the Paths panel that store semi-transparency information.

    D You can create geometric graphics that are easy to draw and modify.

6 You want to create a solid-colored geometric object whose shape you can easily modify later. Which type of tools should you use to create the shape?

    A Vector drawing tools

    B Selection tools

    C Raster drawing tools

    D Pixel-based drawing tools

7 A path's _____ points determine the curvature of its segments.

8 True or false? A path that appears in the Paths panel might contain a secondary path called a subpath.

9 To hide parts of a layer with a vector path, as you would with a layer mask, what should you create?

10 True or false? "Vector mask" and "clipping path" are interchangeable terms.

11 Name three ways to use vector paths that appear directly in the image, not just in the Paths panel.

12 You want to flow type along a curving path. What should you do?

    A Use a Path Type tool.

    B Select the path in the Paths panel, and click with a Type tool at the location where you want to begin adding type.

    C Select a type layer and a shape layer; then choose Layer, Bind Type to Path.

    D You can't flow type along a vector path in Photoshop.

13 You're creating a logo based on type you've entered with the Type tool. You want to use the Direct Selection tool to reshape the characters to add visual interest. What must you do to the type layer before you can reshape the letters with the Direct Selection tool?

A   Choose Layer, Type, Convert to Shape.

B   Choose Layer, Rasterize, Type.

C   Choose Layer, New Layer Based Slice.

D   Choose Layer, Type, Warp Text.

14 How can you save a work path as a permanent path?

A   Create a selection with any selection tool; then choose Make Work Path from the Paths panel menu.

B   In the Paths panel, select the work path and click the "Load path as a selection" icon.

C   In the Paths panel, double-click the work path; then enter a new name and click OK.

D   In the Paths panel, select the work path and click the "Fill path with foreground color" button.

15 How can you convert a selection to a path?

A   Choose Select, Save Selection.

B   Choose Select, Load Selection.

C   In the Paths panel, click the "Load path as a selection" icon.

D   In the Paths panel, click the "Make work path from selection" icon.

Unit 4

Creative image effects

Unit time: 80 minutes

Complete this unit, and you'll know how to:

A Use painting tools, filters, blending modes, and custom brushes to simulate illustrated and painted effects.

B Warp text and layers.

C Group layers and use Smart Objects when creating a composite.

D Edit an image by using the Vanishing Point feature.

E Apply filters as Smart Filters, and mask Smart Filters.

Topic A: Painting effects

This topic covers the following Adobe ACA exam objectives for Photoshop CS5.

#	Objective
3.1b	Demonstrate knowledge of how to organize and customize the workspace.
4.4b	Identify Adjustment menu tools that are used for adjusting tone.
4.5i	Demonstrate knowledge of when to use various blending mode options.
4.6c	Identify tools that are used for painting.
4.6e	Identify the purpose of an option from the Brushes panel.
4.6f	Demonstrate knowledge of color blending.
4.8e	Identify the appropriate filter to use for a variety of situations.

Filters and custom brushes

Explanation

In addition to adjusting photographic images to retain a realistic appearance, you can apply Photoshop's filters to make a photograph look more like a painting or sketch. You can use a filter along with blending modes to simulate the texture of a canvas or other painting surface, and you can create custom brushes for "stamping" repeats of images or creating realistic-looking brush strokes. To simulate brush strokes in an image, you might use the Mixer Brush tool instead of a filter.

The Mixer Brush tool

The Mixer Brush is a new tool in Photoshop CS5 that you can use to simulate realistic painting effects. You can mix colors in an image, combine colors on a brush, and vary the "wetness" of paint across a stroke.

The Mixer Brush tool is located in the group with the Brush tool. When it's selected, you can use the new Brush Presets panel to select a brush that simulates several kinds of paintbrushes. You can fine-tune a brush's settings in the Brush panel. After selecting a brush preset, you specify settings on the options bar, as shown in Exhibit 4-1, to control how the brush interacts with the colors in an image.

To paint with the Mixer Brush:

1 If desired, create a new layer in order to preserve the original image.
2 Select a brush from the Brush Presets panel.
3 Specify the desired settings in the Brush panel.
4 Set the brush size.
5 Load paint into the brush reservoir by sampling color from the image:

- Press and hold I to temporarily select the Eyedropper tool. Click to sample a single color.
- Press Alt and click to sample a range of colors in the image.

6 To automatically load the selected color into the brush with each stroke, click the Automatic Load button.

7 To automatically clean the brush after each stroke, click the Automatic Clean button.

8 From the brush combination presets list, select a preset to automatically specify settings for Wet, Load, Mix, and Flow. Adjust these settings as desired.

- **Wet** — Determines how "wet" the colors in the image will appear when you paint, simulating wet paint on a canvas. If this value is high, the brush will produce longer streaks.

- **Load** — Determines how much paint is loaded onto the brush from the color you sample. If this value is low, the brush will "dry out" faster.

- **Mix** — Determines how much paint is mixed from the canvas to the brush. If this value is low, more color from the brush will be painted onto the image; if it's high, more color from the image will be used.

- **Flow** — Determines the rate at which paint is applied to the canvas.

9 To interact with colors from layers other than the current layer (for example, when painting on an empty layer), check Sample All Layers.

10 Paint with various strokes in the image.

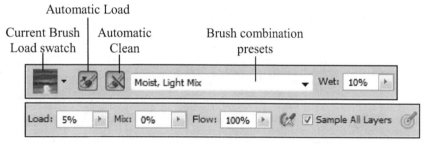

Exhibit 4-1: Mixer Brush settings on the options bar (shown in two parts)

If you select the Automatic Load button, Photoshop will load the brush with the color you selected after each stroke; if this button isn't selected, Photoshop will clear the brush color after each stroke. Likewise, if you select the Automatic Clean button, Photoshop will clean the brush after each stroke; otherwise, the brush will pick up color from the image, simulating a paint brush with which you've painted on a wet canvas. You can load and clean the brush manually at any time by selecting an option from the Current Brush Load list.

The History panel and the Art History Brush tool

You can also paint in an image by using the History Brush tool or the Art History Brush tool to paint with pixels from a state in the History panel. The History Brush tool paints pixels into an image exactly as they appear in the specified state or snapshot in the History panel. The Art History Brush tool paints the pixels from the specified history state but with a simulated painting style.

To paint pixels from a history state into the current image:

1 In the History panel, click to the left of the state or snapshot whose pixels you want to paint into the image.

2 Select the History Brush tool or the Art History Brush tool.

3 If you're using the Art History Brush tool, select a style from the Style list on the options bar.

4 Drag in the image to paint pixels from the specified history state.

Do it!

A-1: Simulating painting with the Mixer Brush tool

The files for this activity are in Student Data folder **Unit 4\Topic A**.

Here's how	Here's why
1 Open Sunset 1	
Save the image as **My sunset 1**	In the current topic folder.
2 From the Workplace switcher menu, choose **Painting**	
3 Press (SHIFT) + (CTRL) + (N)	You'll paint on a new layer in order to preserve the original image.
Name the new layer **Painted**	
4 In the Tools panel, click and hold [brush icon]	(The Brush tool.) To display tools grouped with the Brush tool.
Select the **Mixer Brush** tool	
5 In the Brush Presets panel, scroll and select the indicated brush

Round Fan Stiff Thin Bristles. |
On the options bar, from the preset list, select **Moist, Light Mix**	
Check **Sample All Layers**	To sample colors from the Background layer, rather than from just the current layer (which is empty.)
Set the brush size to **30**	Use the Brush Preset picker, or press [or].
Verify that the Automatic Load and Clean buttons are selected	
6 Press (ALT) and click in the top-left corner of the image	To sample multiple colors from the sky. The colors are loaded in the brush.
On the options bar, observe the Current Brush Load swatch

To see the colors currently loaded in the brush. |
| Drag from left to right across the top of the image | To create brush strokes. |

7 Brush twice more across the sky	To fill the sky with brush strokes. Don't brush over the sun yet.

8 Press (ALT) and click in the clouds	To load a new set of colors into the brush.
Using a combination of short strokes and circular motions, paint across the clouds	To create a "fluffy" effect. Don't paint over the sun yet.
9 Press (ALT) and click in the sun	
Using a circular motion, paint over the sun	

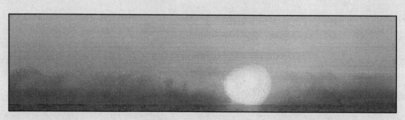

10 In the Brush Preset panel, select the indicated brush	

Round Blunt Medium Stiff.

11 Press (ALT) and click in the ocean	
Using a combination of strokes, paint over the ocean	To create the desired effect. Don't paint over the sun's reflection yet.
12 Continue sampling image areas and painting	Until the entire image has a painted appearance.
13 Hide and show the Painted layer	To see the effect of the Mixer Brush tool.
14 Update the image	

Simulating a textured surface

Explanation

When you modify a photographic image to make it look like a painting or sketch, you might want to simulate the appearance of a textured surface. For example, you might want to make your image look like it's painted onto a textured canvas. You can create a variety of textures by using the Texturizer filter.

If you apply the Texturizer filter directly to the layer containing your image pixels, the effect permanently changes those pixels. If you apply the texture to an additional layer, however, you can continually adjust how the image and the texture interact. To make the textured layer appear on the image pixels, apply the Overlay blending mode.

Using an Overlay-neutral color

In *Overlay blending mode*, middle gray is a neutral color. Pixels in the overlay layer that are darker than middle gray will darken the layer below, and pixels that are lighter than middle gray will lighten the layer below. Middle-gray pixels won't alter the appearance of the pixels in the layer below. When you apply a Texturizer filter to an Overlay blending-mode layer, the filter will darken and lighten parts of the underlying layers, creating an effect similar to applying the filter directly to the underlying layers.

Creating a texture effect by using Overlay mode

To create a texture effect by using Overlay mode:

1. Open the New Layer dialog box:
   - Press Alt and click the "Create a new layer" button.
   - From the Layers panel menu, choose New Layer.
2. In the Name box, enter a layer name.
3. From the Mode list, select Overlay.
4. Check "Fill with Overlay-neutral color (50% gray)."
5. Click OK.
6. Choose Filter, Texture, Texturizer to open the Filter Gallery dialog box with the Texturizer options showing.
7. Specify the texture settings you want, and click OK.

The texture won't appear over white or black pixels in the layer below. If you need to lighten or darken pixels in the layer below to convert white or black areas into light or dark gray, so the texture appears in those areas, you can add a Levels adjustment layer above it. Drag the output sliders to adjust the colors, and click OK.

Do it!

A-2: Blending a texture with Overlay mode

Here's how	Here's why
1 Press (ALT) and click 🔲 in the Layers panel	(The "Create a new layer" button.) To open the New Layer dialog box.
Name the layer **Canvas**	
From the Mode list, select **Overlay**	
Check **Fill with Overlay-neutral color (50% gray)**	
Click **OK**	A gray-filled layer appears in the Layers panel, but there is no effect on the image because in Overlay mode, 50% gray is an invisible effect.
2 Move the layer to the top of the stacking order	If necessary.
3 Choose **Filter, Texture, Texturizer...**	To open the Filter Gallery dialog box with the Texturizer settings showing.
Click **OK**	To use the default canvas texture.
4 Select the Painted layer	You'll use a Levels adjustment to make the colors appear richer.
Create a Levels adjustment layer	(In the Layers panel, click the "Create new fill or adjustment layer" button and choose Levels from the pop-up menu.) To open the Adjustments panel.
Drag the black input slider to **25**, as shown	To increase the intensity of the dark tones in the image.
5 Update and close the image	

Custom brushes

Explanation

You can create a brush from any image source up to 2500 × 2500 pixels, and you can specify whether the brush will create a continuous flow of paint or a series of "stamped" versions of the image.

To design a custom brush:

1 If you want the brush to have varying opacity levels, make the design either color or grayscale. The lighter the pixels in the original image, the less opaque those pixels will be within the brush.

2 Select the design with any selection tool. To create a hard-edged brush, set feathering to zero; to create soft edges, use higher feathering values.

3 Choose Edit, Define Brush Preset.

4 If you want to change brush settings—such as spacing, shape dynamics, and scattering—and save them as part of a preset, first select a brush tool and change the settings in the Brushes panel. Then, from the Brushes panel menu, choose New Brush Preset.

5 If you've changed settings and want to delete the original custom brush you created, click Brush Presets and do either of the following:

• Hold Alt and click the original custom brush.

• Select the brush. Then either right-click it and choose Delete, or choose Delete Brush from the panel menu.

Do it!

A-3:   Creating a custom brush

The files for this activity are in Student Data folder **Unit 4\Topic A**.

Here's how	Here's why
1 Open Star anise	You'll create a custom brush from this star shape.
2 Select the Elliptical Marquee tool	
Create a circular marquee around the star shape, as shown	
	Hold Alt as you drag from the center outward, and hold Shift to constrain the marquee to a circular shape. Move the marquee, if necessary, by pressing Spacebar.
3 Choose **Edit**, **Define Brush Preset...**	To open the Brush Name dialog box.
Edit the Name box to read **Star anise**	
Click **OK**	To create the preset.
Close the image	Next, you'll test the brush in a new image.
4 Create a 600px × 600px image with a white background	Choose File, New; enter 600 in the Width and Height fields; select White from the Background Contents list; and click OK.
Save the image as **Star anise brush strokes**	In the current topic folder.
5 Select the Brush tool	
Press D	To set the foreground and background colors to their defaults of black and white.
From the Brush Preset picker, select the **Star anise** brush	The Star anise brush is the last item in the list.
Drag in the image to paint with the Star anise brush	
	The repeating brush shapes overlap one another and appear in grayscale, not in the original star anise colors. You'll change settings to make the brush appear to stamp individual repeats of the star anise, rather than creating overlapping ones.

6 Open the Brush panel	Click its icon in the panel dock.
Select the **Brush Tip Shape** category	If necessary.
Drag the Spacing slider to **120%**	Any value over 100% creates individual "stamps," with space between them.
Drag to paint in the image	To test the setting. Next, you'll make the shapes vary in size and rotation as you drag.
7 In the Brush panel, select the **Shape Dynamics** category	
Drag the Size Jitter slider to **25%**	To vary the size automatically.
Set the Angle Jitter to **50%**	To make the angle vary randomly.
Drag to paint in the image	

The star anise stamp now varies in size and angle. You'll save these settings in a new preset.

8 From the Brush panel menu, choose **New Brush Preset...**	To open the Brush Name dialog box.
Edit the Name box to read **Star anise stamp**	
Click **OK**	To create the preset. Next, you'll eliminate the original preset you created.
9 In the Brush Presets panel, press (ALT) and point to the Star anise brush	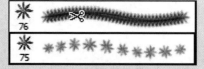

To access the Delete cursor.

While still pressing (ALT), click the Star anise brush	To delete it.
10 Close the Brush panel	
Switch to the **Essentials** workspace	
Update and close the image	

Topic B: Warping

This topic covers the following Adobe ACA exam objective for Photoshop CS5.

#	Objective
4.3e	Demonstrate knowledge of how to reposition or warp image elements.

Warped text and images

Explanation

You can reshape text, layer content, or selections by applying a *warp*. You can warp items to apply a variety of creative effects.

Warped text

You can warp Photoshop text to reshape it for a variety of effects. Warping text reshapes the text characters and flows the text along a curving baseline. After you apply a warp, the text remains editable as text. To warp text:

1   In the Layers panel, select the type layer.
2   Select either the Horizontal or Vertical Type tool.
3   On the options bar, click the Create warped text button to open the Warp Text dialog box.
4   From the Style list, select a warp style to preview its effect on the text on the selected layer. You can press Down Arrow to select each warp style in the list.
5   Select Horizontal or Vertical to specify the direction in which the style will affect the text.
6   Specify Bend, Horizontal Distortion, and Vertical Distortion values to control how the warp style will affect the text.
7   Click OK.

Do it!

B-1: Warping text

The files for this activity are in Student Data folder **Unit 4\Topic B**.

Here's how	Here's why
1 Open Zesty 1	
Save the image as **My zesty 1**	In the current topic folder.
2 Select the Zesty! layer	In the Layers panel.
3 Select the Horizontal Type tool	
On the options bar, click 🔲	(The Create warped text button.) To open the Warp Text dialog box.
4 From the Style list, select **Arc**	
Observe the text in the image	The text now flows along a curved baseline.
Press ⬇ several times to view each style	
5 From the Style list, select **Bulge**	
Set the Bend value to **+55**	
Set the Horizontal Distortion value to **-33**	
Set the Vertical Distortion value to **0**	If necessary.
6 Click **OK**	

Warping images

You can also warp image content. You can warp a selection or an entire layer by applying a preset warp or creating a custom warp.

To warp a selection or layer:

1   Create a selection, or select a layer in the Layers panel. (To select a layer, you can click it in the Layers panel, or press Ctrl and click any of the layer's content in the image window.)

2   Choose Edit, Transform, Warp to add a warp grid to the selection or layer.

3   Apply a preset warp, a custom warp, or both.

  • Drag the grid handles to warp the selection.

  • On the options bar, select a preset warp from the Warp list. To further customize the preset warp effect, select Custom from the Warp list and drag the grid handles.

4   Press Enter to apply the warp.

You can use the Edit, Transform, Warp command and the Warp list on the options bar to apply a preset warp to a type layer. However, you can't apply a custom warp to a type layer.

Do it!

B-2: Warping image layers

Here's how	Here's why
1 Select the Move tool	
2 Press (CTRL) and click the red pepper in the image	To select the Red pepper layer. You'll experiment with an unrealistic, cartoonish distortion of the red pepper to create a fun, playful image.
Press (CTRL) + (J)	To create a duplicate layer.
Name the layer **Red pepper warped**	
Hide the Red pepper, Red pepper shadow, and Pattern Fill 1 layers	
3 Choose **Edit**, **Transform**, **Warp**	A warp grid appears on the pepper.
On the options bar, from the Warp list, select **Fish**	To distort the pepper.
Drag the top-left handle of the grid down slightly, as shown	To adjust the curvature.
4 From the Warp list, select **Custom**	
5 Point within the grid as shown	Notice that the mouse pointer changes shape.

6 Drag down and to the left, as
   shown

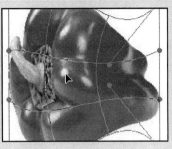

To further distort the image.

7 Drag the direction handle,
   extending from the top-right
   corner of the warp mesh, as
   shown

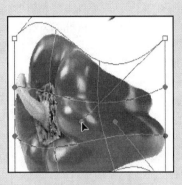

8 Press ⏎ ENTER   To complete the warp.

9 Choose **Edit**, **Transform**,   A grid with even squares appears. You can't
   Warp   access a warp's original grid or clear an image
                                     warp after committing it.

   Press ESC   To clear the grid.

10 Press CTRL and click the word   To select the type layer.
   Zesty! in the image

   Choose **Edit**, **Transform**,   Warp settings appear on the options bar.
   Warp

   Scrub the V value to **-12**

                                     On the options bar.

   Press ⏎ ENTER   To complete the warp.

11 Show the Pattern Fill 1 layer

   Update and close the image

Puppet Warp

Explanation

Another tool you can use to warp an image with even more control is Photoshop CS5's new Puppet Warp command. Using this command, you can transform and distort image areas while leaving other parts of the image intact. For example, you can use Puppet Warp to straighten a curved road or to rotate a subject's arm or leg while leaving the rest of the body unmoved.

To use Puppet Warp:

1 Select the layer containing the object you want to warp.

2 Choose Edit, Puppet Warp. A mesh appears over the contents of the layer.

3 On the options bar, select the desired settings, as shown in Exhibit 4-2:

- **Mode** — Determines the overall elasticity of the mesh.

- **Density** — Determines the spacing of the mesh. For more precise warping, select More Points, but be aware that this can increase processing time.

- **Expansion** — Expands or contracts the outer edge of the mesh in relation to the layer contents.

4 Click to place pins in the mesh at areas you want to transform and at areas you want to remain fixed. To delete a pin, select it and press Delete, or press Alt and click it. To delete all pins, click the Remove all pins button on the options bar.

5 Click to select a pin, and drag it to transform the image.

6 On the options bar, from the Rotate list, select either Fixed or Auto to rotate the mesh based on the selected mode.

7 If desired, rotate the mesh around specific points. To do so, first select the point. Then press Alt and point just outside of the point. When a circle appears, drag to rotate the mesh.

8 When the transformation is finished, press Enter or click the Commit Puppet Warp button.

Exhibit 4-2: Puppet Warp settings on the options bar

By using Puppet Warp, you can overlap parts of an image, but you might want part of an image to appear behind, rather than in front of, another part (or vice versa). You can adjust this by selecting a pin and, on the options bar, clicking the Pin Depth buttons.

While the Puppet Warp mesh is visible, you can press Ctrl+Z to undo the last transformation. Because individual transformations don't appear in the History panel, you can't undo more than one transformation. You can, however, undo all transformations by pressing Esc. Once you've committed Puppet Warp transformations, you won't be able to undo them by, for example, moving part of the image that you've overlapped with another part, because these transformations alter the image pixels.

Puppet Warp works best if the image you want to warp is on a separate layer. That way, you can adjust an object without having to pin many other image areas that you want to remain fixed.

Do it!

B-3:   Using Puppet Warp

The files for this activity are in Student Data folder **Unit 4\Topic B**.

Here's how	Here's why
1 Open Puppet	
Save the image as **My puppet**	In the current topic folder.
2 Select the Manikin layer	If necessary.
3 Choose **Edit**, **Puppet Warp**	To display a mesh over the layer.
On the options bar, from the Density list, select **More Points**	To increase the density of the mesh, allowing for more control over the warp.
4 Observe the mesh	It extends slightly beyond the image
On the options bar, edit the Expansion box to read **0**	
5 Observe the pointer	It indicates that clicking will add pins to the image.
Click as shown	To add a pin to the manikin's head. When you point to a pin, the pointer changes to indicate that you can drag the pin to warp the mesh. However, you first need to add other pins.
6 Click to add pins to the indicated areas	

7   Click the indicated pin

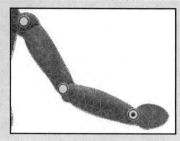

To select it.

From the Rotate list, select **Fixed**

Drag the pin up, as shown

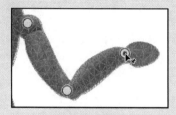

To rotate the manikin's arm at the elbow.

8   On the options bar, from the Rotate list, select **Auto**

Photoshop automatically adjusts the mesh to compensate for the rotation.

Press and hold (ALT) and point just outside of the indicated pin

A circle indicates that you can rotate the mesh.

While holding (ALT), drag to rotate the hand, as shown

9   Click the elbow pin and rotate the arm up toward the manikin's head

As you drag, the elbow moves but the hand stays fixed. You want to rotate the entire arm at the shoulder.

Press (ALT) and click the elbow pin

To delete it. The mesh compensates slightly.

10 Click the hand pin and drag the arm as shown

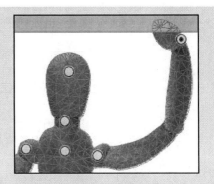

11 Click to add a pin to the elbow again

Drag the hand as shown

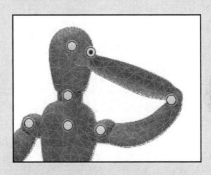

12 Observe the hand	It covers the manikin's head. You want it to appear behind the manikin's head.
On the options bar, click	(The Pin Depth button.) To move the pin down in the stacking order.
Observe the hand	It is now behind the manikin's head.
13 On the options bar, from the Mode list, select **Distort**	To see the effect of this option, which isn't appropriate for this image.
From the Mode list, select **Rigid**	The arm is less distorted than in Normal mode.
14 On the options bar, click ✔	To commit the warp.
15 Update and close the image	

Topic C: Efficient compositing

This topic covers the following Adobe ACA exam objectives for Photoshop CS5.

#	Objective
3.1e	Demonstrate knowledge of non-destructive editing.
3.2a	Identify and label elements of the different types of layers.
3.2e	Demonstrate knowledge of how to create layer groups and links.
3.4b	Identify techniques used to produce reusable images.

Compositing

Explanation

When you create an image by combining images—a process known as *compositing*—you can use several techniques to keep your workflow efficient. For example, you can group layers together to organize the Layers panel and to manipulate multiple layers as a unit. When you select a group, you can move all of its layers as a unit, or adjust the group's blending mode or opacity to apply those settings to all layers in the group.

In addition, when applying transformations and other types of changes to layers, you can make those changes nondestructive by converting layers to Smart Objects. A *Smart Object* is an object that acts as a layer but stores the original image data of one or more layers. Smart Objects allow you to transform an image to smaller sizes and then back to the original size with no loss in quality.

Grouping

You might want to organize image layers into groups. A *group* is a container in the Layers panel that can store layers. You can expand a group so that all of its layers are listed in the Layers panel, or collapse the group to hide its list of layers.

To create an empty group with the default settings, click the "Create a new group" button in the Layers panel. The group will be named Group 1.

To create an empty group with settings you specify:

1 Open the New Group dialog box by doing either of the following:
- From the Layers panel menu, choose New Group.
- Press Alt and click the "Create a new group" button.
2 In the Name box, enter a name for the group.
3 Specify a color for the group icon, and specify a blending mode and opacity for the group.
4 Click OK.

To create a group containing selected layers and using the default settings, first select the layers you want to store in the group. Then drag the selected layers to the "Create a new group" button. The group will be named Group 1.

To create a group containing selected layers and using settings you specify:

1 Select the layers you want to store in the group.

2 Open the New Group from Layers dialog box:

   • From the Layers panel menu, choose New Group from Layers.

   • Press Alt and drag the layers to the "Create a new group" button.

3 Enter a name for the group.

4 Specify a color for the group icon, and specify a blending mode and opacity for the group.

5 Click OK.

To add a layer to a group in the Layers panel, drag the desired layer onto the group. To delete a group, select it and click the Delete layer button. In the alert box that appears, click Group and Contents to delete the group and its layers, or click Group Only to delete the group without deleting the layers within it.

Do it!

C-1: Grouping layers

The files for this activity are in Student Data folder **Unit 4\Topic C**.

Here's how	Here's why
1 Open Zesty 2	
Save the image as **My zesty 2**	In the current topic folder.
2 Select the Red pepper layer	
Press (SHIFT) and click the Chiles shadow layer	To select the range of layers.
3 From the Layers panel menu, choose **New Group from Layers...**	To open the New Group from Layers dialog box.
Edit the Name box to read **Vegetables**	
Click **OK**	To create the group.
4 Verify that the Vegetables group is selected	▷ ▣ **Vegetables**
Using the Move tool, drag in the image	To move all of the layers in the group at once.
Press (CTRL) + (Z)	To undo the move.
5 Lower the opacity of the Vegetables group to **50%**	To change the opacity for all of the layers in the group.
Press (CTRL) + (Z)	To return the group to 100% opacity.

Smart Objects

Explanation

Transforming image content, such as by rotating, scaling, or warping, is typically a destructive edit. A *destructive edit* is one that permanently changes pixel data. Therefore, transforming an image can degrade image quality. For example, if you scale a layer to 25% of its initial size, the layer content is rendered with fewer pixels. If you later scale the layer back to its original size, it will likely appear blurry.

You can transform image content nondestructively by converting it to a Smart Object. A Smart Object stores the original image data and references that data each time you apply a transformation. Therefore, you can transform a Smart Object, and each time, it's as though you're transforming the original image data, as shown in Exhibit 4-3.

Transformed
layer content

Transformed
Smart Object

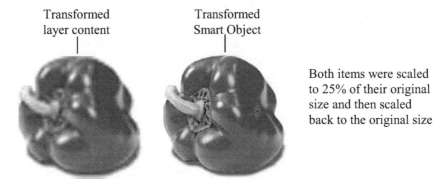

Both items were scaled
to 25% of their original
size and then scaled
back to the original size

Exhibit 4-3: Transformed layer content compared to a transformed Smart Object

Converting layers to Smart Objects

You can convert one or more layers to a single Smart Object. In the Layers panel, a Smart Object looks like a layer, but its thumbnail has a Smart Object badge icon.

To convert to a Smart Object, select the layer or layers you want to convert and choose Convert to Smart Object from the Layers panel menu. The layers appear as a single Smart Object in the Layers panel, and the Smart Object badge appears on the thumbnail.

After converting a layer or layers to a Smart Object, you can transform the Smart Object without cumulatively degrading the image with each new transformation. For example, you can choose Edit, Free Transform to use the Free Transform command to resize objects proportionally.

Do it!   **C-2:   Creating and transforming Smart Objects**

Here's how	Here's why
1 In the Layers panel, click as shown	
	To expand the Vegetables group.
Select the Red pepper and Red pepper shadow layers	Click the Red pepper layer; then Shift+click to select the Red pepper shadow layer.
From the Layers panel menu, choose **Convert to Smart Object**	To convert the two layers into a single Smart Object.
Observe the badge on the Smart Object thumbnail	
	The object appears as one layer.
2 Convert the Garlic and Garlic shadow layers to a Smart Object	Select both the Garlic and Garlic shadow layers, and choose Convert to Smart Object from the Layers panel menu.
3 Convert the Chiles and Chiles shadow layers into a Smart Object	
4 In the Layers panel, select the **Red pepper** Smart Object	
Press (SHIFT) and click the **Chiles** Smart Object	To select all three Smart Objects.
5 Press (CTRL) + (T)	To show the transformation handles in the image.
6 Press (SHIFT) and drag the bottom-right transform handle up and to the left	(Don't release the mouse button until instructed to do so.) To reduce the size of the selected objects proportionally.
When the W and H values on the options bar are about **50%**, release the mouse button	
Press (↵ ENTER)	To complete the transformation.

7 In the Layers panel, select each Smart Object individually, and position the objects as shown

8 Select the Garlic layer

Press ⌨ CTRL + ⌨ T   (Or choose Edit, Free Transform.) You'll rescale the garlic image.

Scale the image to approximately **75%**   (Drag the selection handles.) To enlarge it from its original scale value of 50%.

Press ⌨ ↵ ENTER   To commit the change.

9 Select the Chiles layer

Scale it to approximately **70%**   Press Ctrl+T to free-transform the image.

Rotate the Chiles layer slightly counterclockwise   Choose Edit, Transform, Rotate. Point to just outside the bottom-right corner selection handle, and drag up slightly. Press Enter.

10 Scale the Red pepper image to approximately **65%**

11 Rearrange the three Smart Objects to their approximate positions in step 7

12 Update the image

Smart Object contents

Explanation

After converting one or more layers or other content to a Smart Object, you can still access and modify the original content. In addition, you can export the Smart Object content as a separate file.

Modifying Smart Object contents

If you convert several layers into a single Smart Object, you can still access each original layer and make changes that will be reflected in the Smart Object.

To modify the original content:

1 In the Layers panel, select the Smart Object.

2 From the Layers panel menu, choose Edit Contents. A message box appears, explaining that after changing the Smart Object's contents, you'll have to save them to update the Smart Object.

3 Click OK. The original content that you converted to a Smart Object appears in a new window.

4 Modify the content as needed, and then choose File, Save.

5 Close the window displaying the edited content to return to the original image window. This window now displays the updated Smart Object.

Exporting Smart Object contents

You might want to export Smart Object content as a separate file so you can use it in other images. To do so, right-click a Smart Object in the Layers panel and choose Export Contents from the shortcut menu. In the Save dialog box that opens, enter a name for the exported content, and click Save.

The image is exported as a Smart Object file, which uses the PSB file format. You can place the file in other image files as a Smart Object, or you can open it directly in its own image window.

Do it!

C-3: Working with Smart Object contents

Here's how	Here's why
1 Select the Chiles Smart Object	You'll change the shadow of the chiles to better match the shadows of the other vegetables.
From the Layers panel menu, choose **Edit Contents**	A message box appears, stating that you must choose File, Save to commit your changes after editing the content.
Click **OK**	The chiles and shadow appear in a separate image window.
2 Select the Chiles shadow layer	
With the Move tool selected, press [↓] four times	To increase the distance between the chiles and the shadow.
3 Press [CTRL] + [S]	To save the file.
Close the image	The chiles' shadow more closely matches the shadows of the other vegetables. Next, you'll export the Red pepper and its shadow so that you can use it in other images.
4 Right-click the Red pepper Smart Object	To display the shortcut menu.
Choose **Export Contents...**	To open the Save dialog box. Notice that the file type is PSB. A PSB file can be placed in other images.
Navigate to the current topic folder	Student Data folder Unit 4\Topic C.
Click **Save**	To export the object.
5 Update the image	

Vector Smart Objects

Explanation

Smart Objects can store vector data. If you place an Illustrator file into a Photoshop image, the file is placed as a Smart Object, maintaining the original vector data. Therefore, you can transform and manipulate the placed vector file without having to rasterize it. Because vector images can be scaled up without any loss of image quality or crispness, you can safely scale a vector Smart Object to larger than its original size.

To place a vector file into an image as a Smart Object:

1 Choose File, Place to open the Place dialog box.
2 Select the vector file and click Place. The Place PDF dialog box appears.
3 Click OK and press Enter to display the placed content as a Smart Object.

You can right-click a Smart Object based on an Illustrator file and choose Edit Contents to open the file in Adobe Illustrator, if you have that software on your computer.

Do it!

C-4: Creating vector Smart Objects

The files for this activity are in Student Data folder **Unit 4\Topic C**.

Here's how	Here's why
1 Select the Zesty! layer	You'll place an Illustrator file above the Zesty! layer.
Choose **File, Place...**	To open the Place dialog box.
Select **Outlander logo.ai**	
Click **Place**	The Place PDF dialog box appears.
2 In the Crop To list, select **Art Box**	
Click **OK**	To place the logo.
Press ⏎ ENTER	To commit the change. You'll be able to further transform this Smart Object without degrading the image quality.
3 Scale the logo to about **30%**	
4 Rotate and resize the logo as shown	
	When you place vector art, it's treated as a Smart Object. Therefore, it scales smoothly instead of appearing pixelated, as it would if it were rasterized and enlarged to more than twice its original size.
5 Arrange the objects as shown	

6 Using the Crop tool, crop the
image as shown

7 Update and close the image

Topic D: Vanishing Point

This topic covers the following Adobe ACA exam objective for Photoshop CS5.

#	Objective
4.8g	Demonstrate knowledge of editing images using the Vanishing Point filter.

Perspective planes

Explanation

The Vanishing Point filter makes it easier to work with images that contain perspective planes, like buildings, walls, or any flat surface. You use the Vanishing Point dialog box to define the planes in an image. You can then edit the image with more realistic results because the edits are oriented and scaled to the perspective planes. Photoshop Extended users can also use Vanishing Point to measure objects and angles in an image.

To edit an image with the Vanishing Point filter:

1   If you plan to paste an image into the Vanishing Point dialog box, copy that image.

2   Choose Filter, Vanishing Point to open the Vanishing Point dialog box.

3   Define the four corners of the plane surface.

4   If desired, hold down the Ctrl key and drag from an existing node to create other plane surfaces.

5   Paste the image you copied earlier, if necessary.

6   Edit the image, using the plane surfaces as needed.

You can also fill a selection with another area of an image, maintaining the proper perspective. For example, you might want to remove a window from a brick wall in a building, but using the Clone Stamp tool, the Patch tool, or Content-Aware Fill wouldn't produce the desired result. To fill a selection with another area in the Vanishing Point filter, first select the part of the image you want to fill; then press Ctrl and drag from within the selection to the area with which you want to fill the selection. To copy a selection in perspective, press Alt while dragging.

Do it!   **D-1:   Editing an image with the Vanishing Point filter**

Here's how	Here's why
1 Open Building	
Save the image as **My building**	(In the current topic folder.) You'll use the Vanishing Point filter to add a logo to the side of the building.
2 Open Small logo	First, you'll copy the image that you want to paste into the Vanishing Point dialog box.
Select the logo and copy it	Press (CTRL) + (A) and then (CTRL) + (C).
Close Small logo	To return to My building.
3 Choose **Filter**, **Vanishing Point...**	To open the Vanishing Point dialog box. You'll define the plane surface of the building's front.
4 Click at the upper-left corner of the front wall, as shown	

To define the first corner of this plane.

5 Click at the bottom-left corner, as shown

To define the next corner.

6 Click at the wall's bottom-right corner, as shown

To define the third corner.

7 Click at the wall's top-right corner

To define the final corner. This plane surface is defined. Next, you'll define the plane surface on the left side of the building.

8 Point to the center handle on the left side of the plane you defined

Press and hold (CTRL) and drag to the left

To create a perpendicular plane on the side of the building.

Now that you have defined the plane surfaces, the logo will use that perspective.

9 Press CTRL + V   To paste the logo.

10 Drag the logo to the front wall

The logo uses the building's perspective.

11 Drag the logo to the side wall   The logo uses the perspective of that side of the building.

12 Drag the logo so that it's partially on the front wall and partially on the side

The logo matches both sides' perspectives.

13 Click **OK**

14 Update and close the image

Topic E: Smart Filters

This topic covers the following Adobe ACA exam objectives for Photoshop CS5.

#	Objective
3.1e	Demonstrate knowledge of nondestructive editing.
3.2a	Identify and label elements of the different types of layers.
3.2b	Demonstrate knowledge of masks and modes.
4.8d	Demonstrate knowledge of using Smart Filters.
4.8f	Demonstrate knowledge of Smart Filters and how they enable nondestructive editing.

Nondestructive filters

Explanation

When you apply a filter to an image, the filter changes the pixel data to which it is applied. However, you can apply a filter nondestructively as a *Smart Filter*. You can then experiment with filter settings without destructively changing the actual image pixel data. Therefore, you can easily modify a filter's effects, or you can remove the filter altogether from the image to return to the original image appearance.

If you want to apply a filter to a layer as a Smart Filter, you must first convert the layer to a Smart Object layer. You can then apply almost any Photoshop filter to the Smart Object layer, and it will be applied as a Smart Filter. You can also apply the Shadow/Highlight and Variations adjustments as Smart Filters. However, you can't apply the following filters as Smart Filters:

- Extract
- Liquify
- Pattern Maker
- Vanishing Point

Applying a Smart Filter

If the layer to which you want to apply a Smart Filter is not already a Smart Object layer, select it and choose Filter, Convert for Smart Filters. To apply a Smart Filter, select a Smart Object layer, choose a filter, and specify its settings. The Smart Filter then appears in the Layers panel, as shown in Exhibit 4-4.

Exhibit 4-4: The Ripple filter applied as a Smart Filter to a Smart Object layer

Editing a Smart Filter

After you apply a Smart Filter, you can edit its effects at any time. Each time you adjust the filter settings, the new settings are applied to the original image data because the Smart Filter is applied nondestructively. To edit a Smart Filter's settings, double-click it in the Layers panel to open the filter's dialog box.

Removing a Smart Filter

To remove a Smart Filter, drag it to the Delete layer button in the Layers panel. The Smart Filter will be removed and its effects will no longer apply to the image.

Do it!

E-1: Applying Smart Filters

The files for this activity are in Student Data folder **Unit 4\Topic E**.

Here's how	Here's why
1 Open Puppy 4	
Save the image as **My puppy 4**	(In the current topic folder.) The image contains a single layer. You'll convert the layer to a Smart Object so you can apply Smart Filters.
2 Choose **Filter**, **Convert for Smart Filters**	A dialog box informs you that the layer will be converted to a Smart Object.
Click **OK**	
	The layer icon displays a badge to indicate that it's a Smart Object layer. You can now apply filters as Smart Filters.
3 Choose **Filter**, **Distort**, **Ripple...**	To open the Ripple dialog box.
Drag the Amount slider to approximately **400**	
From the Size list, select **Large**	
Click **OK**	
	The Smart Filter applies to the entire image. Because you applied this filter as a Smart Filter, you can adjust its settings at any time, and the changes will be based on the original image, rather than on the current filtered version of it. Therefore, you can regain earlier image detail that the filter might have obscured.

4 In the Layers panel, double-click **Ripple**	To open the Ripple dialog box.
Drag the Amount slider to approximately **100**	
Click **OK**	More of the original image detail returns. You'll add a second Smart Filter.
5 Choose **Filter**, **Texture**, **Patchwork...**	To open the Filter Gallery dialog box, displaying the Patchwork settings.
Click **OK**	Both Smart Filters are now listed in the Layers panel. You'll remove the Smart Filter you just added.
6 Drag the Patchwork Smart Filter to the Delete layer button	(In the Layers panel.) To delete the Smart Filter. Its effects are no longer applied to the image.
7 Update the image	

Smart Filter masks

Explanation

One of the benefits of Smart Filters is that you can easily mask their effects in an image to control which portion of the image displays the filter effect, and you can edit the mask as often as necessary. When you apply a Smart Filter to a Smart Object, a mask thumbnail appears on the Smart Filters line in the Layers panel. By default, the mask thumbnail is white, indicating that the filter's effects apply to the entire layer. You can work with filter masks, using the same techniques you use to work with layer masks. For example, you can paint on a filter mask with black to hide the filter's effects.

Before you apply a Smart Filter, you can select a portion of a Smart Object layer so that when you apply the Smart Filter, it will automatically create a filter mask based on the selection. The filter mask thumbnail displays white to indicate areas where the filter effect will appear, and black to indicate areas where it won't.

Do it!

E-2: Masking Smart Filter effects

Here's how	Here's why
1 Click the Smart Filters mask thumbnail as shown	
	To select the mask thumbnail so you can edit the mask with painting tools. You'll paint with black to hide parts of the Smart Filter.
2 Select the Brush tool	
3 Press ⓧ	To switch the foreground and background colors so that black is now the foreground color.
4 Open the Brush Preset picker	
Select a soft round brush of any size	
Set the size to approximately **400**	
5 Drag over the puppy	To apply black to the filter mask so that the filter's effect is apparent only around the puppy.
6 Observe the filter mask thumbnail	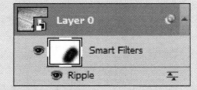
	The thumbnail is black where you painted over the puppy. The thumbnail is white in the surrounding area, so only that part of the image will display the filter's effects.
7 Hide and show the Smart Filters' effects	Click the eye icon next to Smart Filters in the layers panel.
8 Update and close the image	

Unit summary: Creative image effects

Topic A
In this topic, you used the **Mixer Brush tool** to simulate a painted effect. You also applied a **Texturizer filter** to an Overlay blending-mode layer to simulate a textured surface. Finally, you created a **custom brush preset** from a pixel area in an image.

Topic B
In this topic, you used the Create Warped Text button to **warp** a type layer. You also used the Edit, Transform, Warp command to apply a preset warp and to customize a warp. Then you learned how to use the **Puppet Warp** command.

Topic C
In this topic, you **grouped layers** and manipulated them. In addition, you converted layers to **Smart Objects** and transformed them. You also modified the contents of Smart Objects and exported them. Finally, you placed a vector file as a Smart Object.

Topic D
In this topic, you used the **Vanishing Point filter** to edit an image in perspective.

Topic E
In this topic, you converted a layer to a Smart Object, and then you applied a filter as a **Smart Filter**. You also applied a mask to a Smart Filter.

Independent practice activity

In this activity, you'll group layers and convert layer contents to Smart Objects. You'll also paint with the Mixer Brush tool.

The files for this activity are in Student Data folder **Unit 4\Unit summary**.

1 Open Granular spices, and save the image as **My granular spices**.

2 Group the spice and shadow layers for each spice into one new group named **Spices**.

3 Convert each pair (a spice and its shadow) to a Smart Object. Resize them as desired, but don't enlarge past 100%.

4 Place Outlander logo in the image. Put it in the top-left corner of the image at 35% size. (*Hint:* Be sure to commit the resizing and moving actions when you're done.)

5 In a separate step, transform the logo to 60% size.

6 Flatten the image.

7 Paint with the Mixer Brush tool to make the background look as though it were painted. Then update and close the image. (*Hint:* Try using several different brushes to achieve the desired effect.)

8 Open Hawaii logo. Select and copy the image. Then close it.

9 Open Sunset 2, and save the image as **My Sunset 2**.

10 Use the Vanishing Point filter to paste the Hawaii logo in perspective at 50% opacity onto the illuminated portion of the beach, as shown in Exhibit 4-5.

11 Update and close the image.

Exhibit 4-5: The image as it appears after Step 10

Review questions

1 In a layer with Overlay mode applied, what color will appear perfectly transparent to the underlying layer?

2 While using the Mixer Brush tool, you want to load several colors from the image onto the brush. How can you do this?

  A Hold I to select the Eyedropper tool and click in the image.

  B Paint in the image; the brush will pick up colors automatically.

  C Press Alt and click in the image.

  D Press Ctrl and click in the image.

3 How can you create a custom brush based on the current selection?

  A Choose Edit, Define Brush Preset.

  B Choose Edit, Define Pattern.

  C Choose Edit, Preset Manager.

  D Choose Edit, Assign Profile.

4 True or false? After you apply a warp to type, the text remains editable.

5 Which of the following can you apply to a selection or layer? [Choose all that apply.]

  A A preset warp.

  B A custom warp.

  C A preset warp and a custom warp at the same time.

  D None; you can apply a warp only to an entire layer, not to a selection.

6 While using the Puppet Warp tool, you want to delete a pin. Which of the following are methods you can use to do this? [Choose all that apply.]

A Select the pin and press Delete.

B Press Esc.

C Press Alt and click the pin.

D Press Ctrl and click the pin.

7 To organize layers so they appear in a collapsible layer with a folder icon, you should:

A Link them.

B Group them.

C Create a clipping mask.

D Combine them into a Smart Object.

8 Which of the following statements are true of Smart Objects? [Choose all that apply.]

A A Smart Object can be transformed to a small size and then back to its original size with no loss of quality.

B A Smart Object's data cannot be edited after you've converted it from layer data.

C Only raster, not vector, data can be stored as a Smart Object.

D You can combine multiple layers into one Smart Object.

9 How can you convert several selected layers into a Smart Object?

A From the Layers panel menu, choose New Group.

B From the Layers panel menu, choose Convert to Smart Object.

C From the Layers panel menu, choose New Group from Layers.

D From the Layers panel menu, choose Merge Layers.

10 How can you edit an image in perspective?

A Open Vanishing Point and use the rectangle tool to draw a plane.

B Open Vanishing Point and then click to define the four corners of the plane.

C Open the Grid dialog box and drag the grid coordinates to match the plane.

D Choose the Perspective command and drag the grid to align it to the plane.

11 You want to apply a filter to a layer nondestructively. What must you do first?

A Convert the layer to a 3-D object layer.

B Convert the layer to a background layer.

C Convert the layer to a Smart Object layer.

D Convert the layer to an adjustment layer.

12 You've applied the Mezzotint filter as a Smart Filter, and you want to edit the filter settings. How can you open the dialog box to change the filter settings?

A Double-click the Mezzotint layer in the Layers panel.

B Choose Filter, Pixelate, Mezzotint.

C Choose Filter, Mezzotint.

D Double-click the Smart Filters layer in the Layers panel.

Unit 5

Automating tasks

Unit time: 45 minutes

Complete this unit, and you'll know how to:

A Use the Actions panel to record, play, and edit actions.

B Display actions as buttons and organize actions into action sets.

C Run an action on multiple images by batch-processing them.

D Customize keyboard shortcuts and menus.

Topic A: Creating actions

This topic covers the following Adobe ACA exam objective for Photoshop CS5.

#	Objective
4.1g	Identify the methods or commands for undoing a selection.
4.1k	Demonstrate knowledge of batch-processing techniques.

Automation

Explanation

As you work with Photoshop, you might find that you perform certain sets of commands frequently on many images. Photoshop provides several tools for automating repetitive tasks.

For example, you might often open images, apply a particular filter to them, and save them in JPEG format. You can use the Actions panel to create an *action*—a recorded series of operations that can be performed as a single step. You can then run the action at any time on a single image, or you can use a *batch process* to run the action for an entire folder of images.

Another automation tool is the *Image Processor*, which can convert files to JPEG, PSD, and TIFF formats, at specific image sizes. The Image Processor can also run actions.

Additionally, you can run an action on a file, or on all files in a folder, by dragging that file or folder to a droplet. A *droplet* is a small executable file that you create in Photoshop. The droplet can reside anywhere on your PC, such as on the desktop or in a folder. When you drag a file into a droplet, it runs the action or actions that you assigned to that droplet.

Action design

When you create actions, be careful to create action steps that will work with a variety of images. For example, if you want an action to double the width of the image in pixels, you should record the action with the Image Size dialog box set to 200% width. This would double the size of any image to which the action is applied, regardless of the original width. If instead you recorded the action on an image that was 300 pixels wide, and you specified a width of 600 pixels in the Image Size dialog box, then all images you applied the action to would be sized to 600 pixels wide, which wasn't your original intent.

Creating an action

The Actions panel includes some default actions that you can use right away. However, you'll probably need to create your own actions to streamline your specific workflows. To create an action, you can use the Actions panel, shown in Exhibit 5-1, to record a set of commands and steps as you perform them.

To create an action:

1 Open an image that will serve as a good example of the type of images to which you'll apply the action.

2 Perform any steps necessary to prepare this image, but which you don't want to record as part of the action.

3 In the Actions panel, click the Create new action button to open the New Action dialog box.

4 Enter a name for the action, specify a keyboard shortcut for running the action, and choose a color for the action's button (for when you display the Actions panel in Button mode).

5 Click Record.

6 Perform the commands and other steps you want the action to record.

7 In the Actions panel, click the Stop playing/recording button to stop recording action steps.

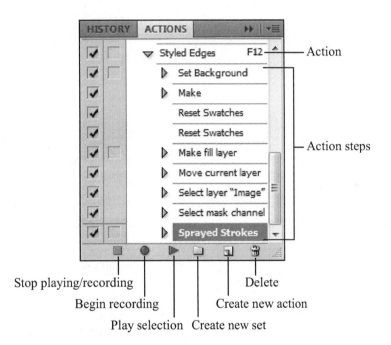

Exhibit 5-1: The Actions panel

Do it!

A-1:   Recording an action

The files for this activity are in Student Data folder **Unit 5\Topic A**.

Here's how	Here's why
1 Open Mountain lake	
Save the image as **My mountain lake**	(In the current topic folder.) You'll use this image to record an action that creates a white, stylized frame around an image.
2 Verify that the rulers are displayed	Before recording the action, you'll create a selection, which the action will use to create a layer mask. Because the layer mask will be a different size and shape for each image that you apply the action to, you won't record creating the selection as part of the action.
3 Using the Rectangular Marquee tool, create a selection as shown	
	(Select the Rectangular Marquee tool and select Normal from the Style list on the options bar.) There should be one inch outside the selection on all sides.
4 Open the Actions panel	
In the Actions panel, click 🔲	(The Create new action button.) To open the New Action dialog box.
5 Edit the Name box to read **Styled Edges**	
From the Function Key list, select **F12**	
From the Color list, select **Red**	
Click **Record**	The next steps you perform in the image will be recorded as steps in the action you just created.
6 Double-click the **Background** layer	To open the New Layer dialog box.
Edit the Name box to read **Image** and click **OK**	You can now manipulate the layer as a regular layer.

7 In the Layers panel, click ⬕ | (The Add layer mask button.) To add a layer mask using the selection.

   Press ⓓ | To set the foreground and background colors to their defaults. You will add a solid-color fill layer that will eventually be used as the background.

8 In the Layers panel, click ⬕ and choose **Solid Color...** | To open the Color Picker.

   In the Tools panel, click the white color swatch |

   Click **OK** | To create a solid-white fill layer.

9 Move the Color Fill 1 layer below the Image layer |

10 In the Image layer, select the layer mask thumbnail |

11 Choose **Filter**, **Brush Strokes**, **Sprayed Strokes...** | To open the Sprayed Strokes dialog box.

   Set the Stroke Length value to **11** |

   Set the Spray Radius value to **25** |

   In the Stroke Direction list, verify that **Right Diagonal** is selected |

   Click **OK** | To apply the filter.

12 In the Actions panel, click ▣ | (The Stop playing/recording button.) To stop recording the action.

13 Drag the bottom edge of the Actions panel down | To enlarge it so you can see all of the steps in the action you just recorded.

14 Update and close the image

Running actions

Explanation

After creating an action, you can run it on other images to perform its steps as a single command, automating your work.

To run an action on a single image:

1 Open the image to which you want to apply the action.
2 Perform any steps necessary to prepare the image for the action.
3 Play the action:

- In the Actions panel, select the action you want to apply and click the Play selection button.
- Press the keyboard keys you assigned to the action.

Do it!

A-2:   Playing an action

The files for this activity are in Student Data folder **Unit 5\Topic A**.

Here's how	Here's why
1 Open Zesty 1	
Save the image as **My Zesty 1**	(In the current topic folder.) Because you created the action after selecting an image area, you could select any image area with any selection tool, and the action would be applied based on that selection.
2 Using the Elliptical Marquee tool, create a selection around the word and vegetables, as shown	
3 In the Actions panel, select **Styled Edges**	
Click ▶	(The Play selection button.) To run the action, which creates the stylized edge.
	The action steps run, but the image layers prevent the effect from being displayed properly.
4 In the History panel, select **Open**	To undo the previous steps.

Editing actions

Explanation

After you create an action and run it on several images, you might find that it doesn't work the way you intended for all images. In addition, you might want to adjust some of the action settings to create a slightly different result. You can modify an action by adding, removing, and modifying steps.

To record a new step for an existing action:

1 In the Actions panel, select the step that you want the new step to follow.
2 Click the Begin recording button.
3 Select the command or perform the step you want to add.
4 Click the Stop playing/recording button.

If you want to change the placement of the added step (in the sequence of steps), you can drag it in the Actions panel.

To modify dialog box settings for an action step:

1 In the Actions panel, select the step you want to modify.
2 From the Actions panel menu, choose Record Again to open the dialog box associated with the selected step.
3 Specify the new settings you want the step to use.
4 Click OK.

To remove an action step, select it and click the Delete button; then click OK.

Do it! **A-3: Editing an action**

Here's how	Here's why
1 In the Actions panel, select the **Set Background** step	You've seen that this action won't work properly on layered images, so it needs a step to flatten the image. You'll record a new step here to flatten the image before continuing.
2 Click ◉	The Begin recording button.
From the Layers panel menu, choose **Flatten Image**	
Click ◼	To stop recording the action. The newly recorded Flatten Image step appears after the Set Background step, but needs to come before it.

Drag the **Flatten Image** step above the Set Background step	▽ Styled Edges F12
	  ▷ ⟨image⟩
	  ▷ Set Background
	  Flatten Image
	  ▷ Make

3 Choose **File**, **Revert**	To revert to the saved image.
4 Create an elliptical selection as shown	
Run the Styled Edges action	(Press F12.) This time, the action works properly. Next, you'll lower the Spray Radius in the Filter Gallery and add another filter to make the effect more interesting.
5 In the History panel, select **Layer Order**	The next-to-last History step.
In the Layers panel, select the layer mask thumbnail for the Image layer	

6   In the Actions panel, select the
    Sprayed Strokes step

    From the Actions panel menu,   To open the Sprayed Strokes dialog box.
    choose **Record Again...**

    Set the Spray Radius value to **23**

7   Click 🔲   The New effect layer icon, located in the
                                          bottom-right area of the dialog box.

    Under Brush Strokes, select
    Spatter

    Set the Spray Radius value to **8**

    Set the Smoothness value to **4**

8   Verify that the Spatter effect is
    above the Sprayed Strokes effect
    in the list

👁	Spatter
👁	Sprayed Strokes

    Click **OK**   To finish re-recording the step.

9   In the Actions panel, expand the   Because this step sets the color to Red 255,
    Make fill layer step   Green 255, Blue 255, it's unnecessary to have a
                                          Reset Swatches step in the beginning of the
                                          action. Therefore, you should delete that step so
                                          the user doesn't lose the active foreground and
                                          background colors.

10 Select the **Reset Swatches**
    step

    Click 🗑   (The Delete button.) An alert box appears.

    Click **OK**   To delete the action step.

11 In the History panel, select
    Elliptical Marquee

12 Play the **Styled Edges** action

13 In the History panel, select **Open** To undo the previous steps.

Pausing actions

Explanation

Some actions might be hard for someone other than the author to run without an explanation or specific setup instructions. You can insert a message, called a *stop*, to explain the purpose of the action, the type of image for which it was intended, or any steps the user should take before running it. In addition, for steps that use dialog box values, you can specify that the dialog box opens during the action's playback so the user can customize settings for that step each time the action is used.

To pause an action and insert a stop:

1 In the Actions panel, select the action to which you want to add a stop.

2 From the Actions panel menu, choose Insert Stop to open the Record Stop dialog box.

3 In the Message box, enter the message that you want Photoshop to display when the action is played.

4 Check Allow Continue if you want users to be able to ignore the message and continue running the action. If you clear Allow Continue, the user will be forced to click Stop, stopping the action's playback. The user can then continue playing the action, however, beginning with the step following the Stop step.

For steps that require dialog box settings, you can have the dialog box open during the action's playback. The user can then specify settings for that step, customizing the action each time it's used. To have a step's associated dialog box open during playback, click the "Toggle dialog on/off" column next to that step, as shown in Exhibit 5-2.

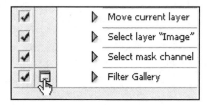

Exhibit 5-2: The "Toggle dialog on/off" column

Do it!

A-4: Pausing an action

Here's how	Here's why
1 Run the Styled Edges action	Because you haven't made a selection , an alert box states that some steps will not run properly.
Click **Stop**	To stop playback. You'll add a step that displays a message telling the user to make a selection before running the action, and warning the user that running the action will flatten the image.
2 Revert the image	Choose File, Revert.
3 Select the **Styled Edges** action	

4   From the Actions panel menu,   To open the Record Stop dialog box.
    choose **Insert Stop...**

    In the Message box, enter
    **This action requires a selection. If you haven't made a selection,
    please do so. It also flattens the image, so create a duplicate if
    you want to retain the original layers.**

    Check **Allow Continue**   To allow users to either stop the action's
                                        playback or continue playing the action.

    Click **OK**   To create the Stop step.

5   Move **Stop** to the first step in the
    action, as shown

6   Click the "Toggle dialog on/off"
    column for the Filter Gallery step,
    as shown

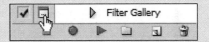

                                        The dialog box associated with this step will
                                        open when you play the action, allowing you to
                                        change settings each time you run the action.

7   Run the Styled Edges action   The action stops, and a dialog box appears with
                                        the message you specified.

    Click **Stop**   So you can specify a selection.

8   Create an elliptical marquee

9   Run the Styled Edges action   The alert message appears again.

    Click **Continue**   At the Filter Gallery step, the Filter Gallery
                                        dialog box opens.

    Click **OK**   To complete the action playback.

10 Update and close the image

Topic B: Organizing actions

This topic covers the following Adobe ACA exam objective for Photoshop CS5.

#	Objective
4.1k	Demonstrate knowledge of batch-processing techniques.

Methods of organizing actions

Explanation

You might want to organize your actions to make them easier to find and run. You can organize actions into folders called *action sets*, or you can display actions as a group of buttons in the Actions panel.

Button mode

By default, the Actions panel displays actions as a list. In a list, you can expand an action to display its steps. You can also set the Actions panel to display the actions as buttons.

When you use Button mode, the actions appear as colored buttons, as shown in Exhibit 5-3. You can then run an action by clicking the button, rather than by selecting the action's name and clicking the Play selection button. In addition, you'll be able to find an action more quickly because the individual steps don't appear.

To display the Actions panel in Button mode, choose Button Mode from the Actions panel menu. To return to the default mode, display the Actions panel menu and choose Button Mode again to uncheck it.

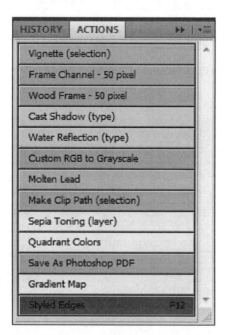

Exhibit 5-3: The Actions panel in Button mode

Do it!

B-1: Making actions work as buttons

The files for this activity are in Student Data folder **Unit 5\Topic B**.

Here's how	Here's why
1 Open Zesty 2	
Save the image as **My zesty 2**	In the current topic folder.
2 From the Actions panel menu, choose **Button Mode**	To display the actions in the panel as buttons.
3 Select an area of the image	
4 Click **Styled Edges**	To run the action.
Respond to each dialog box that appears	To finish running the action.
5 Update the image	

Action sets

Explanation

By default, all actions are stored in an action set named Default Actions. You can create additional action sets to organize your actions into categories.

Organizing actions into sets makes it easier to find an action. You can collapse the action sets you don't need at the moment and expand just the one containing the actions you want, making the Actions panel less cluttered. When you display the Actions panel in Button mode, the buttons from all action sets are displayed together.

Creating action sets

To create an action set, use either of these techniques:

- In the Actions panel, click the Create new set button to create a set named Set 1. Rename the action set by double-clicking its name and entering a new one. (The Create new set button isn't available in Button mode.)
- From the Actions panel menu, choose New Set to open the New Set dialog box. Enter a name and click OK.

To add an action to a set, drag the action to the set's folder icon in the Actions panel.

Sharing actions

After creating actions, you can share them with other Photoshop users. To share the actions in an action set:

1. In the Actions panel, select the action set containing actions you want to share.
2. From the Actions panel menu, choose Save Actions to open the Save dialog box.
3. Click Save to save the action set as a file.
4. Copy the saved action-set file to another computer where you want to use it.
5. Start Photoshop. From the Actions panel menu, choose Load Actions to open the Load dialog box.
6. Select an action-set file and click Load to add it to the Actions panel.

Do it!

B-2: Saving actions in sets

Here's how	Here's why
1 From the Actions panel menu, choose **Button Mode**	To turn off Button mode. You'll duplicate the Styled Edges action and modify the duplicate to add a white fill layer behind other layers. This technique is convenient for creating effects such as silhouettes.
2 Click the arrow to the left of the Styled Edges action	To collapse the steps.
Drag the **Styled Edges** action to the Create new action icon	To create a duplicate. The duplicate is named "Styled Edges copy."
Double-click the name **Styled Edges copy**	To select it.
Type **White fill layer background** and press ⏎ ENTER	To rename the duplicate action.

3 Expand the "White fill layer background" action	You'll delete all of the steps except the ones to make a white fill layer and to move the layer to the back.
Press (CTRL) and click each action step, *except* for Make fill layer and Move current layer	To select the steps.
Click 🗑	A dialog box appears, asking you to verify that you want to delete these steps.
Click **OK**	To remove the selected steps.
4 Collapse the steps for the "White fill layer background" action	Click the triangle to the left of the name.
5 In the Actions panel, click ▭	(The Create new set button.) To open the New Set dialog box.
In the Name box, enter **My Actions**	
Click **OK**	To create the set.
6 Drag the **Styled Edges** action to the My Actions folder icon	To add the action to the set.
Add the **White fill layer background** action to the set	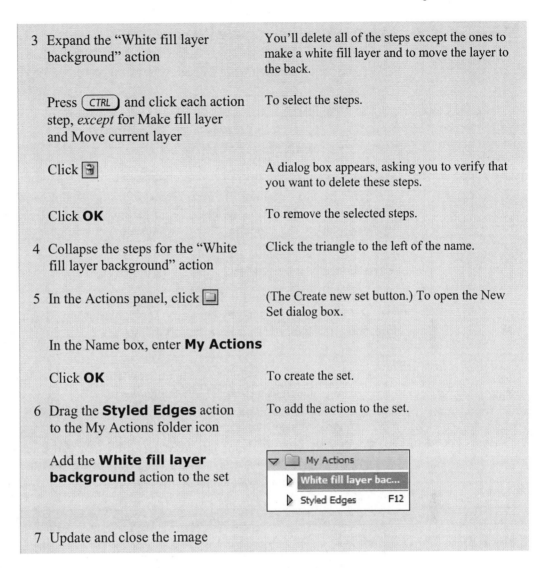
7 Update and close the image	

Topic C: Batch processing

This topic covers the following Adobe ACA exam objective for Photoshop CS5.

#	Objective
4.1k	Demonstrate knowledge of batch-processing techniques.

Explanation

You might want to run an action on several images. For example, you might create an action to size images uniformly for printing or for the Web. It would be tedious to apply such actions to each image individually; instead, you can *batch-process* them to let Photoshop apply the action to all of them in sequence without your intervention.

The Batch command

To perform a batch process in Photoshop, choose File, Automate, Batch. In Bridge, you can perform a batch process by choosing Tools, Photoshop, Batch. In the Batch dialog box, shown in Exhibit 5-4, select the following:

- The action you want to run.
- The source from which to draw images. The source can be a folder, an import source (such as a scanner), files open in Photoshop, or selected files in Bridge. You can specify whether to include subfolders in the selected folder and how to handle issues that arise when images are opened.
- The destination in which to save the results. You can save and close the original file or save the results in a folder. You can specify how the batch process should name files and how it should handle errors that occur when the action is run.

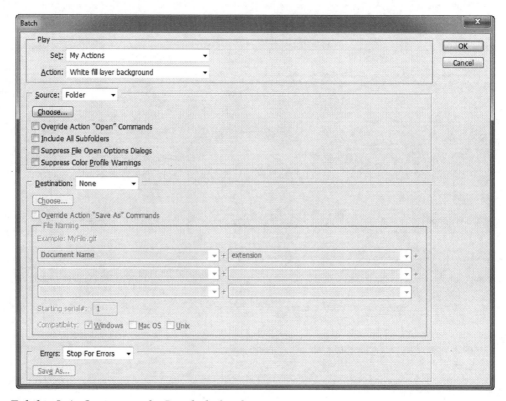

Exhibit 5-4: Options in the Batch dialog box

Do it!   **C-1:   Batch-processing files**

The files for this activity are in Student Data folder **Unit 5\Topic C**.

Here's how	Here's why
1 From the Scenic photos folder, open Hawaii photo	
Observe the Layers panel	The image has only one layer.
Close Hawaii photo	You'll add a white fill layer to each of the files in the Scenic photos folder to prepare them for masking areas with a white background.
2 Choose **File**, **Automate**, **Batch...**	To open the Batch dialog box.
3 From the Set list, select **My Actions**	(If necessary.) The action to add the fill layer is in the set you created.
4 From the Action list, select **White fill layer background**	If necessary.
5 From the Source list, select **Folder**	(If necessary.) To run the action on all of the images in a selected folder.
Click **Choose**	To open the Browse for Folder dialog box.
Browse to the **Scenic photos** folder in the current topic folder	
Click **OK**	To select the Scenic photos folder.
6 From the Destination list, select **Save and Close**	To make the batch process store the results of the action in the original files it opens.
7 Click **OK**	To run the batch process on the Scenic photos folder.
8 Open Hawaii photo	
Observe the Layers panel	
	The image now contains a Color Fill 1 layer behind the original Photo layer. At this point, you could run a new action on this and other images, with the fill layer having been created.
9 Close Hawaii photo	

Topic D: Customizing Photoshop

This topic covers the following Adobe ACA exam objective for Photoshop CS5.

#	Objective
3.1b	Demonstrate knowledge of how to organize and customize the workspace.

Customizing keyboard shortcuts and menu colors

Explanation

It's a good idea to memorize the keyboard shortcuts for commands you use often. In addition, you can create keyboard shortcuts for commands that don't have default shortcuts. You can also customize the appearance of menu commands to make it easier to find the ones you need.

Customizing keyboard shortcuts

To assign a keyboard shortcut:

1 Open the Keyboard Shortcuts and Menus dialog box:
   - Choose Edit, Keyboard Shortcuts.
   - Choose Window, Workspace, Keyboard Shortcuts & Menus and then click the Keyboard Shortcuts tab.
2 Expand the category containing the command you want.
3 Click the command for which you want to add a keyboard shortcut.
4 With the Shortcut box activated, press the keys you want to assign as the shortcut. If another command is already using the shortcut, assigning it to the current command will remove it from the previous command.
5 Click Accept.

After customizing keyboard shortcuts, you can save the current assignments as a keyboard shortcut set. That way, you can create multiple sets for yourself and other users. To switch among shortcut sets, open the Keyboard Shortcuts and Menus dialog box and select the desired set from the Set list. If you want to return to the default set of keyboard shortcuts, choose Window, Workspace, Reset Keyboard Shortcuts.

Customizing menu command colors

You can use the Keyboard Shortcuts and Menus dialog box to customize the appearance of commands in the menu bar. You can specify that a particular menu item not appear in the menu, or you can apply a color to a menu item. Adding color to some menu items can make it easier to find the commands you use most often.

To customize the appearance of menu-bar items:

1 Open the Keyboard Shortcuts and Menus dialog box:

- Choose Edit, Menus.
- Choose Window, Workspace, Keyboard Shortcuts & Menus and then click the Menus tab.

2 Expand the category containing the command you want to customize.

3 Click the command whose appearance you want to customize.

4 Specify options for the item's appearance.

- To hide the item (so it won't appear in the menu), click the eye icon in the visibility column.
- To change the item's color, click in the Color column to open the Color list, and select the desired color.

5 Click OK.

As with keyboard shortcuts, you can save your menu customizations as a set, and you can switch among sets, depending on your needs. To return to the default set, choose Window, Workspace, Reset Menus.

Do it!

D-1: Assigning keyboard shortcuts and menu item colors

Here's how	Here's why
1 Choose **Edit, Keyboard Shortcuts...**	To open the Keyboard Shortcuts and Menus dialog box with the Keyboard Shortcuts tab active.
2 Expand the Window category	You'll assign a keyboard shortcut to the History command in the Window menu so you can quickly show and hide the History panel.
Scroll in the commands list until you see History	
3 Select **History**	The Shortcut box for the History command is active.
Press F9	An alert box states that F9 is already in use and that assigning it to this command will remove it from the Window, Actions command.
Press ALT + SHIFT + F9	This keyboard shortcut is not being used by any other command.
Click **Accept**	You will save the modified keyboard shortcuts in a new set.
4 Click 🖫	To open the Save dialog box.
Edit the File name box to read **Action editing shortcuts**	
Click **Save**	To save the set.
5 Click the **Menus** tab	You will apply a color to several menu items to make them easier to see.
Expand the Window category	
6 Select **Actions**	
In the Color column next to Actions, click **None**	To display the Color list.
From the Color list, select **Red**	
Apply the Red color to the **History** menu item	

7 Click 🖺   To open the Save dialog box.

Name the set
Action editing menus

Click **Save**

Click **OK**

8 Click the **Window** menu   Observe that the Actions and History commands
                                        are red, and the new keyboard shortcut appears
                                        next to the History command.

Close the menu

Unit summary: Automating tasks

Topic A   In this topic, you recorded an **action** to automate a multiple-step procedure. You also ran an action and modified action steps. Finally, you added **stops** to an action and specified that certain dialog boxes appear during an action's playback.

Topic B   In this topic, you displayed actions as **buttons** and clicked an action button to play it. You also organized actions into **action sets**.

Topic C   In this topic, you used a **batch process** to run an action on multiple files.

Topic D   In this topic, you created **keyboard shortcuts** for commands and specified colors for menu items.

Independent practice activity

In this activity, you'll create an action, edit the action steps, and run the action.

1 Create an image with pixel dimensions of 400×400 with a transparent background.

2 Add a layer to the image (so you can eventually record an action step to bring a layer to the front after you create a layer that's not in front). Select the bottom layer.

3 Create an action named **Star field** that contains the following steps:
   a Create a layer and then choose Layer, Arrange, Bring to Front.
   b Choose Select, All. Choose Edit, Fill; select Black as the fill color; and click OK. Deselect the selection.
   c Choose Filter, Noise, Add Noise; specify an amount of **16**; select Gaussian distribution; check Monochromatic; and click OK.
   d Choose Edit, Transform, Scale. On the options bar, click the link icon between the W and H boxes to make them both change when you enter a value. Enter **200** in the W box, and press Enter twice.
   e Choose Image, Adjustments, Levels, and specify Input levels of **40**, **0.70**, and **140**.

4 Stop recording.

5 Before the Levels step, add a stop with the text **Drag the midtone slider to change star density**. Allow users to continue.

6 Toggle the dialog box on for the Levels step.

7 Duplicate the Levels step. (*Hint:* Drag it to the Create new action button.)

8 Create an image with pixel dimensions of 800×800, and run the Star field action. When the Message dialog box appears, click **Continue**. In the Levels dialog box, drag the midtone slider to specify the midtone you want, and click **OK**. In the second Levels dialog box that appears, drag the midtone slider, and click **OK** to finish running the action.

9 Close all images without saving them.

10 Close Photoshop.

Review questions

1 You've created an action to share with colleagues, but you realize that they might not understand that they need to make a selection specific to the image before running the action. How can you verify that they'll see this information every time the action is run?

A Insert a stop by selecting the action and choosing Insert Stop from the Actions panel menu.

B Insert a stop by selecting the action and choosing Insert Menu Item from the Actions panel menu.

C In the Actions panel, click the "Toggle dialog on/off" column next to the first step.

D It's not possible to do this in Photoshop. You'll have to notify your colleagues in some other way.

2 Which of the following are possible sources for images you want to batch-process? [Choose all that apply.]

A A folder of files, including the contents of subfolders

B Selected files in Adobe Bridge

C Multiple folders stored in different locations on your computer

D Files already open in Photoshop

3 How can you run an action on multiple files at once?

A Run the action from the Actions panel.

B Run the action in Button mode.

C Choose File, Automate, Batch.

D Drag the files to the Actions panel.

4 True or false? A batch process must store the results of the action in another location, not in the original files.

5 True or false? You can change the colors of menu items.

6 How can you customize keyboard shortcuts?

A Choose Edit, Preferences.

B Choose Edit, Menus.

C Choose Edit, Keyboard Shortcuts.

D Right-click a command, enter the keyboard shortcut you want it to use, and click OK.

7 How can you customize menus by using the Menus tab in the Keyboard Shortcuts and Menus dialog box? [Choose all that apply.]

A You can move commands from one menu to another.

B You can specify that a menu command be displayed in a particular color.

C You can specify that a menu command no longer appear in the menu.

D You can choose a new font for all menu commands.

Course summary

This summary contains information to help you bring the course to a successful conclusion. Using this information, you will be able to:

A Use the summary text to reinforce what you've learned in class.

B Determine the next courses in this series (if any), as well as any other resources that might help you continue to learn about Photoshop CS5.

Topic A: Course summary

Use the following summary text to reinforce what you've learned in class.

Unit summaries

Unit 1

In this unit, you added colors to the **Swatches panel** and used fill shortcuts to fill selections and layers with color. You also used **fill layers** to create layers filled with solid color. In addition, you learned how to add a **gradient** to a layer or selection and how to create a gradient fill layer. Next, you created and applied a fill by using **patterns**. You also saved a set of color swatches as a **preset** and saved tool presets. Finally, you learned how to use **overlay layer styles**.

Unit 2

In this unit, you painted in **Quick Mask mode** to add to and subtract from a selection, and you painted in an **alpha channel** to modify a selection. You also created and modified a **layer mask** to hide part of a layer. Next, you created **grayscale masks** to partially mask a portion of an image. Finally, you applied a **clipping mask** and used the Horizontal Type Mask tool to create a mask from text.

Unit 3

In this unit, you learned about **vector paths**. You drew paths, converted selections to paths, and saved paths. In addition, you used the Direct Selection tool to **edit paths**, added and removed anchor points, and created **subpaths**. Next, you used **vector masks** to mask layer content and designated a path as a **clipping path**. You also converted type to paths and **wrapped type along a path**. You then added **shape layers** to an image and applied layer styles to the shapes. Finally, you created brush strokes that flowed along the shape of a path.

Unit 4

In this unit, you used the **Mixer Brush tool** to simulate a painted effect and applied a **Texturizer filter** to an Overlay blending-mode layer. Then you created a custom brush preset from a pixel area in an image. You also learned how to **warp** a type layer, apply a preset warp, customize a warp, and use the **Puppet Warp** command. In addition, you **grouped layers** and manipulated them. You also learned how to work with **Smart Objects**. Next, you used the **Vanishing Point filter** to edit an image in perspective. Finally, you worked with **Smart Filters**.

Unit 5

In this unit, you learned how to record, run, modify, and pause an **action**. You also learned how to display actions as buttons and how to organize actions into action sets. Next, you used a **batch process** to run an action on multiple files. Finally, you created **keyboard shortcuts** for commands and specified colors for menu items.

Topic B: Continued learning after class

It is impossible to learn how to use any software effectively in a single day. To get the most out of this class, you should begin working with Photoshop CS5 to perform real tasks as soon as possible. We also offer resources for continued learning.

Next courses in this series

This is the second course in this series. The next course in this series is:

- *Photoshop CS5: Production, ACA Edition*

Other resources

For more information, visit www.axzopress.com.

Photoshop CS5: Advanced, ACA Edition

Glossary

Action

A saved series of steps that Photoshop can perform in sequence with a single click in the Actions panel.

Action set

A group of actions stored as a file, which you can distribute to other users.

Alpha channel

An additional channel that does not contribute to the image itself, as do color channels.

Anchor points

Points that a vector path flows through, much like the dots in a connect-the-dots drawing.

Batch process

The process of running an action on multiple images, with the results stored either with the original image files or as new files in a specified folder.

Clipping mask

A mask that uses the content of one layer to hide part of the content in another layer. The transparent space in the layer below specifies the areas that are masked in the layer above.

Clipping path

A vector path that determines which parts of an image should be transparent when the image is placed in a document in another application.

Compositing

Combining multiple images, often for the purpose of creating a new, realistic-looking image.

Corner point

An anchor point on a vector path in which two segments flow in different directions. The direction points for a corner point don't have to face exactly opposite one another.

Direction point

A point that extends from an anchor point on a vector path and determines the curvature of the adjoining segment.

Droplet

An applet that you can drop files into, to be processed. A droplet can be generated by Photoshop. It is stored on the computer desktop or in a folder, and it runs a specified action.

Fill layer

A special type of layer that can contain a solid color, a gradient, or a pattern, and that automatically expands to fill the image if you change its canvas size.

Flatness value

A value that designates how many small straight segments a PostScript printer should use in simulating a smooth curve. The higher the value, the fewer the segments.

Gradient

A blend of two or more colors in which the colors fade gradually from one to another.

Group

A container in the Layers panel that can store multiple layers so you can manipulate them together and collapse them to one item in the panel.

HSB color model

A three-channel color model that defines colors based on their hue, saturation, and brightness.

Image Processor

An automation tool that can convert an image to a PSD, JPEG, or TIFF file, resize the image, and run an action against that image.

Layer mask

A grayscale component that's added to a layer to designate each pixel's visibility. A black pixel in a layer mask makes the corresponding image pixel invisible; a white layer-mask pixel makes the image pixel fully visible.

Masking

Selecting pixels for the purpose of partially or fully obscuring them from view.

Overlay

A fill, gradient, or pattern applied to a layer through a layer style.

Pattern

A saved rectangular design of pixels that you can use for filling or painting as adjacent tiles in an image.

Preset

A stored swatch, gradient, pattern, brush, style, contour, custom shape, or tool setting. Photoshop comes with presets, and you can create your own.

Quick Mask mode

A mode that displays a selection as a semi-transparent overlay to help you differentiate between selected and non-selected image areas.

Segment

The part of a vector path between two anchor points.

Shape layer

A layer consisting of a fill and a vector mask, which creates the appearance of a filled shape within the mask's edges.

Smart Filter

A filter applied to a Smart Object layer so that the filter is applied nondestructively.

Smart Object

An object that acts as a layer but stores the original image data of one or more layers. Smart Objects allow you to transform an image to smaller sizes and then back to the original size with no loss in quality.

Smooth point

An anchor point on a vector path in which the segments on either side curve in the same direction. Smooth points have direction points that face exactly opposite one another.

Stop

An action step that pauses the action and displays a message to the user.

Subpath

A secondary path created along with another path in the Paths panel. Subpaths can add to, subtract from, intersect with, or exclude original path areas, depending on the option selected.

Swatch

A color saved in the Swatches panel.

Vector mask

A vector path component added to a layer to designate each pixel's visibility, much like a layer mask does.

Vector path

A geometric shape, such as a smoothly flowing curve, defined by a series of points with segments between them.

Warp

A transformation you can apply to text or image layers that reshapes the content. You can create warps based on preset shapes or by dragging handles.

Work paths

Paths that make no visible change in the image but can be used to create vector paths, selections, or clipping paths.

Index